PIANO · VOCAL · GUITAR

2nd EDITION

THE BEST EARLY ROCK 'N' ROLL SONGS EVER

ISBN 978-0-634-03755-9

Visit Hal Leonard Online at
www.halleonard.com

CONTENTS

ARE YOU SINCERE

Words and Music by WAYNE WALKER
and LUCKY MOELLER

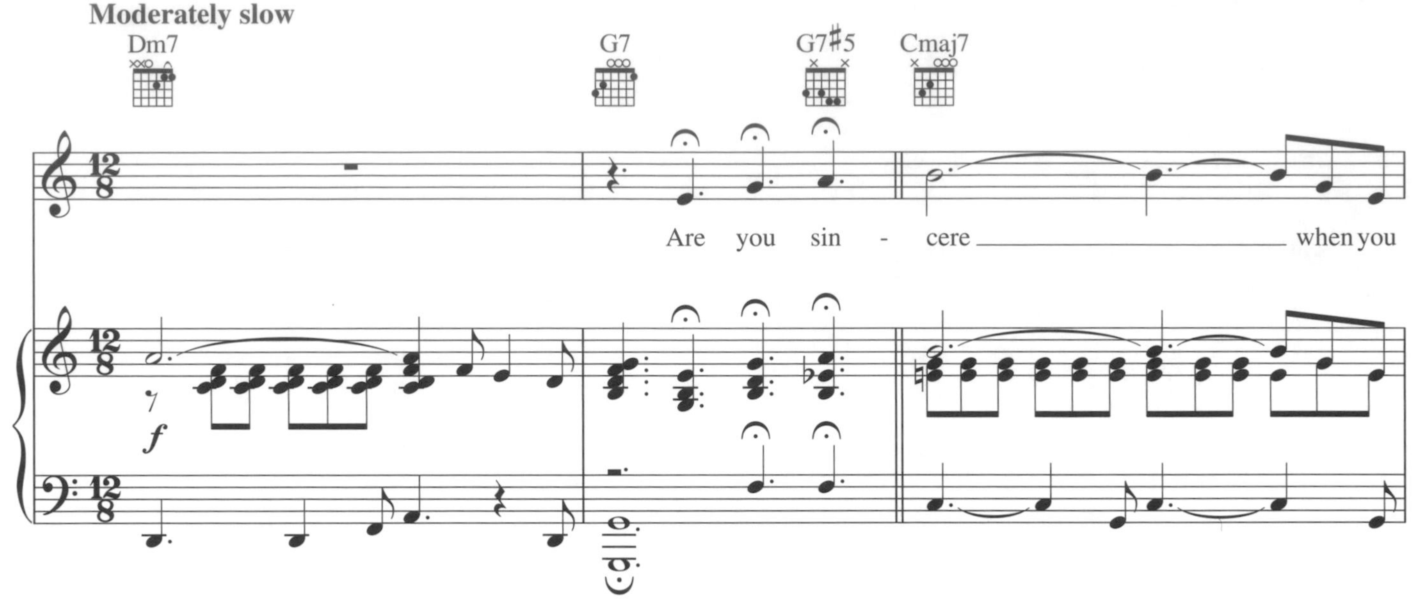

G7
true?"
Do you
C
Am
C7
mean
ev - 'ry
word
that
F6
Fm
F
my
ears
have
heard?
I'd like
to
know
which way
to
C
Am7
Dm7
G7
C
F
go,
will our
love
grow,
are you
sin -
cere?

C N.C. Cmaj7 Dm7

Are you sin - cere when you say you

G7 G7♯5

miss me? Are you sin -

Cmaj7 Dm7

cere ev - 'ry time you

G7 C

kiss me? And are you real-ly

Am
C7
F6
mine ev - 'ry day, all the
Fm
F
C
Am7
time? I'd like to know which way to go, will our love
Dm7
G7
C
grow? Are you sin - cere?
F
C
C6/9

BE-BOP-A-LULA

Words and Music by TEX DAVIS
and GENE VINCENT

C N.C. C N.C. C N.C. C N.C.
She's the gal in the red blue jeans. She's the queen of all the teens.
She's the one that's got that beat. She's the one with the fly - in' feet.
C N.C. C N.C. C N.C.
She's the one that I know. She's the one that loves me so.
She's the one that walks a - round the store. She's the one that gets more and more.
F7 C
Be-bop - a - lu - la, she's my ba - by. Be-bop - a - lu - la, I don't mean may - be.
G7 F7/G C
1 2
Be bop-a - lu - la, she's my ba - by doll, my ba-by doll, my ba-by doll. doll.
rit.

BOOK OF LOVE

Words and Music by WARREN DAVIS,
GEORGE MALONE and CHARLES PATRICK

Dm
Gm7
C7
I love you, dar - ling,
ba - by, you know I do,
but I've
F
Dm
Gm7
C7
F
got to see this book of love,
find out why it's true;
I won - der, won - der
B♭
F
who,
who,
who wrote the book of love?
B♭
F
B♭
Chap - ter One says to love her,
to love her with all your heart;
Chap - ter Two you

C7
F
tell her you're nev - er, nev - er, nev - er, nev - er ev - er gon - na part. In Chap - ter Three re -
Dm
Gm7
C7
F
mem - ber the mean - ing of ro - mance; in Chap - ter Four you
Dm
Gm7
C7
F
break up, but you give her just one more chance. Oh, I won - der, won - der
B♭
F
who, who, who wrote the book of love?

Dm
Gm7
C7
Baby, baby, baby, I love you, yes, I do; well, it
F
Dm
Gm7
C7
says so in this book of love, ours is the one that's true. I
F
B♭
wonder, wonder who, who, who wrote the book of
1
F
love?
2
F
love?
sf

BREAD AND BUTTER

Words and Music by LARRY PARKS
and JAY TURNBOW

C F C F C F
That's what my ba - by feeds me. I'm her lov - in'
C
man.
Chorus
F
1.,4. He likes bread and
2.,3. No more bread and
C F C F C F
but ter, he likes toast and jam.
but - ter, no more toast and jam.
C F C F
That's what his ba - by feeds him.
He found his ba - by eat - in'

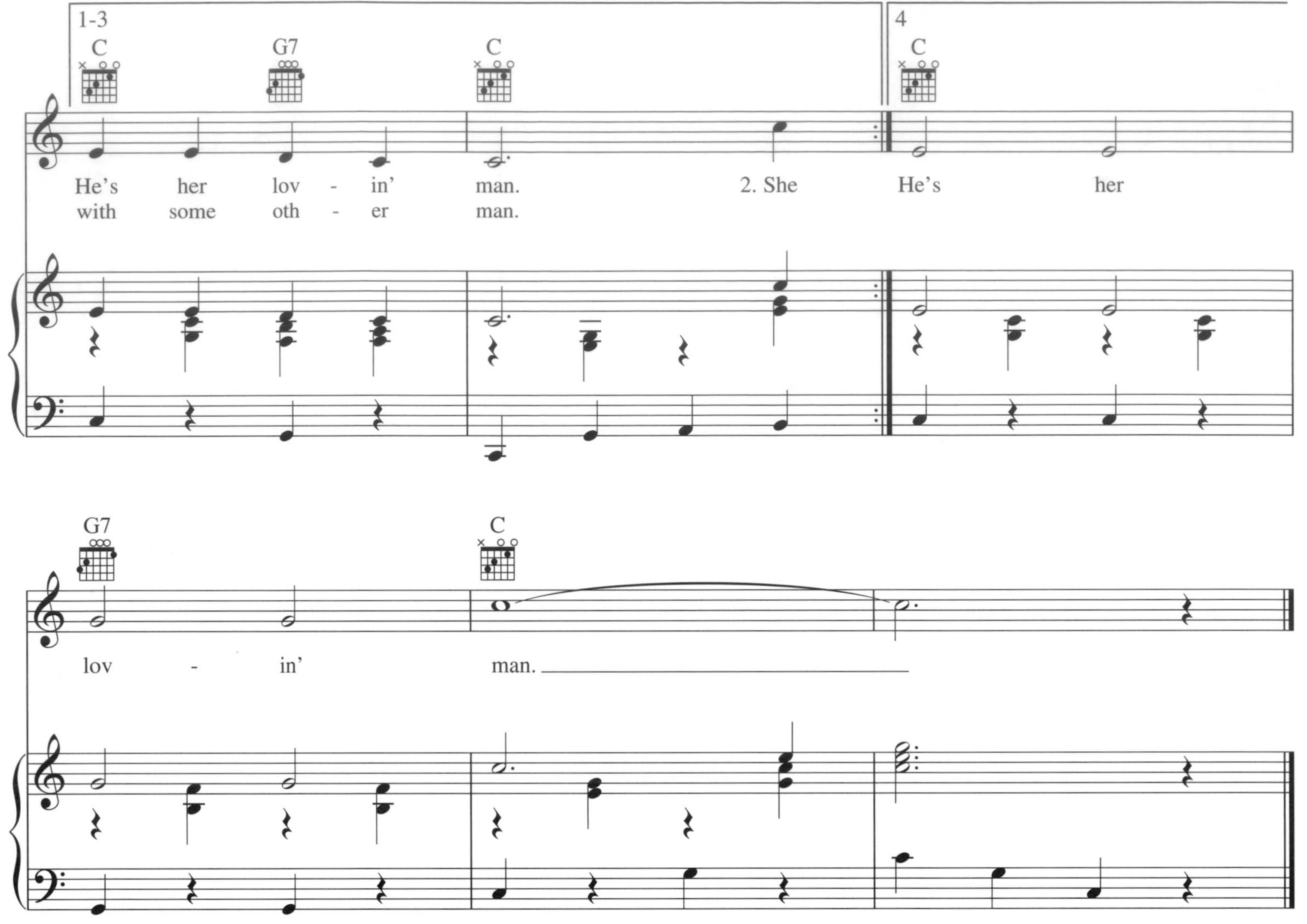

Additional Lyrics

2. She don't cook mashed potatoes,
   Don't cook T-bone steak,
   Don't feed me peanut butter,
   She knows that I can't take...
   Chorus

3. Got home early one mornin',
   Much to my surprise
   She was eatin' chicken and dumplin's
   With some other guy.
   Chorus

4. No more bread and butter,
   No more toast and jam.
   I found my baby eatin'
   With some other man.
   Chorus

CATHY'S CLOWN

Words and Music by
DON EVERLY

C7
F
B♭
F
by, then he's not a man at all.
bad, or don't you e - ven care?
Don't want your
love
an - y -
more.
Don't want your kiss -
- es, that's for sure.
I die each

Dm
B♭
time
I hear this sound.
C7
F
Here he comes.
That's Cath - y's
1
clown.
When you see me shed a
2
clown.

CAN'T HELP FALLING IN LOVE

from the Paramount Picture BLUE HAWAII

Words and Music by GEORGE DAVID WEISS,
HUGO PERETTI and LUIGI CREATORE

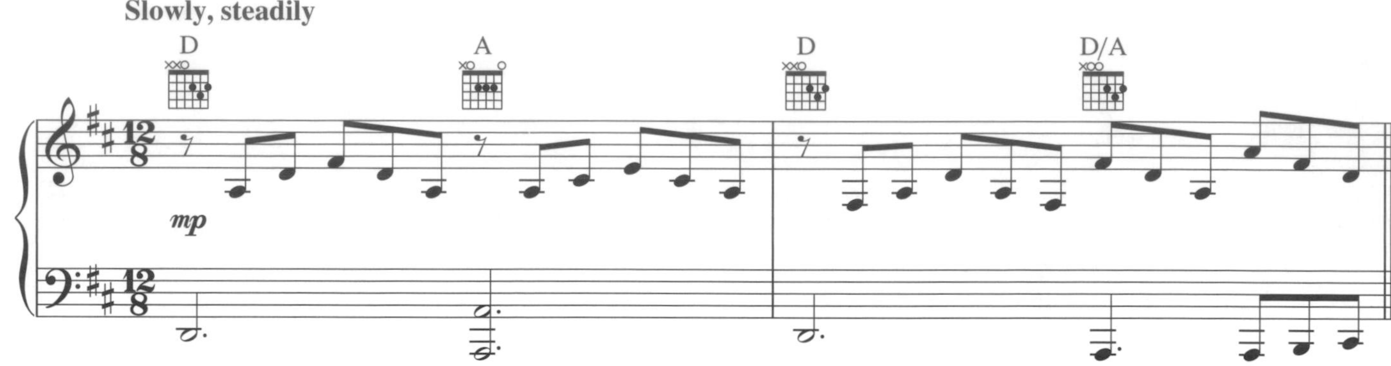

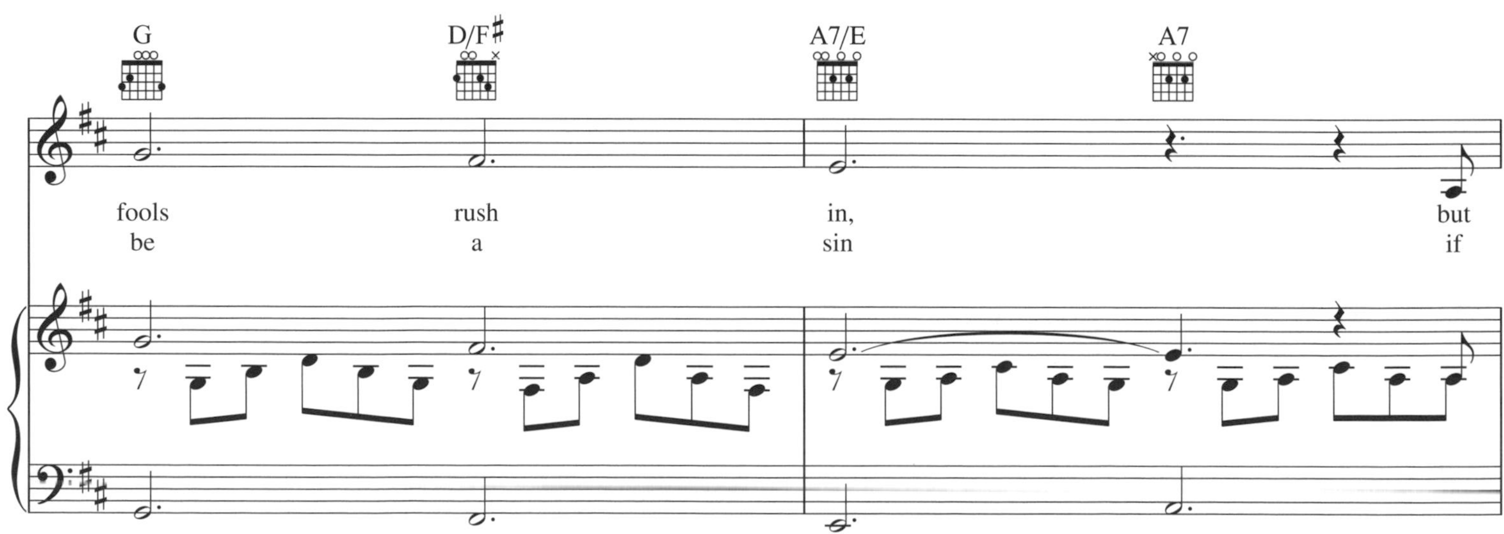

G
A
Bm
G6
Em
I can't help fall - ing in
I can't help fall - ing in
D/A
A7
1
D
D/A
love with you.
love with
2
D
F♯m
C♯
you?
Like a riv - er flows
F♯m
C♯
F♯m
C♯
sure - ly to the sea,
dar - ling, so it goes;

F♯m
B7
Em
A7
some things are meant to be.
D
F♯m
Bm
Take my hand, take my
G
D/F♯
A7/E
A7
whole life, too, for
G
A
Bm
G6
Em
I can't help fall - ing in

1
D/A
A7
D
D/A
love with you.
2
D
G
A
you. For I can't
Bm
G6
Em
D/A
A7
help fall - ing in love with
rit.
D
you.

CHARLIE BROWN

Words and Music by JERRY LEIBER
and MIKE STOLLER

F
Bb/C
F
clown that Char - lie Brown He's
C7
Bb7
To Coda
gon - na get caught just you wait and see
F
1
(Spoken:) "Why is ev - 'ry - bod - y al - ways pick - in' on me?" That's
(Tacet when sung
2
Bb7
pick - in' on me?" Who's al - ways

writ - in' on the walls?
A♭7
4fr
Who's al - ways goof - in' in the halls?
B♭7
Who's al - ways throw - in' spit - balls?
C7
Guess who "Who

me?" Yeah you! Who
F
walks in the class - room cool and slow?
F7
D.S. al Coda
Who calls the Eng - lish teach - er dad - dy - o? Char - lie
CODA
F
"Why is ev - 'ry - bod - y al - ways pick - in' on me?"
(Tacet when sung

CRYING

Words and Music by ROY ORBISON
and JOE MELSON

C
G7
wished me well; you could - n't tell that I'd been
don't love me and I'll al - ways be
C
Em
C
cry - ing o - ver you, cry - ing
cry - ing o - ver you, cry - ing
Em
F
o - ver you. When you said, "So
o - ver you. Yes, now you're
G7
F
G7
long;" left me stand - ing all a - lone, a - lone and
gone and from this mo - ment on I'll be

C
C+
F/C
cry - ing, cry - ing, cry - ing,
cry - ing, cry - ing, cry - ing,
Fm/C
C
cry - ing. It's hard to un - der - stand, but the
cry - ing. Yeah, cry - ing,
G7
1
C
touch of your hand can start me cry - ing.
cry - ing o - ver
2
C
I thought that you.

DA DOO RON RON
(When He Walked Me Home)

Words and Music by ELLIE GREENWICH,
JEFF BARRY and PHIL SPECTOR

B♭
C
F6
name was Bill. Da doo ron ron ron, da doo ron ron.
my oh my. Da doo ron ron ron, da doo ron ron.
make him mine. Da doo ron ron ron, da doo ron ron.

F
B♭
F
Yes, my heart stood still. Yes, his
Yes, he caught my eye. Yes, but
Yes, he looked so fine. Yes, I'm gon - na

C7
F
B♭
name was Bill.
my oh my.
make him mine.
And when he walked me home, da

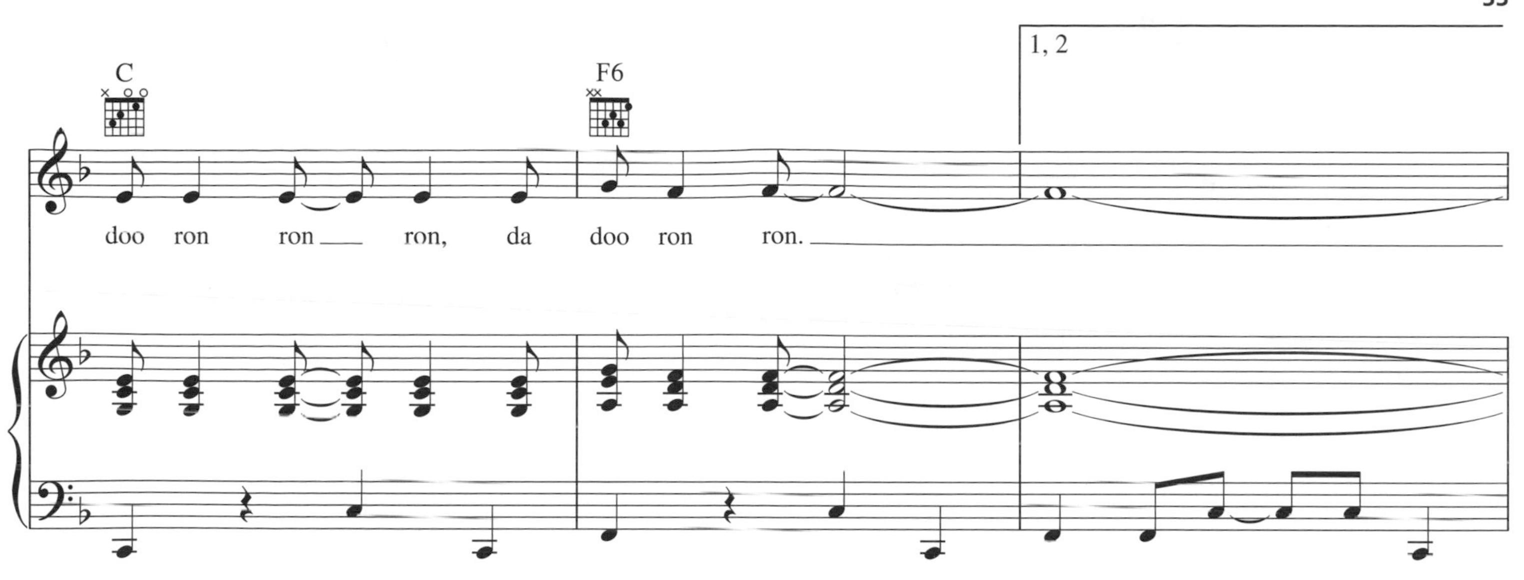
C
F6
1, 2
doo ron ron ron, da doo ron ron.

3
F
He
He
Yeah, yeah. Yeah,

B♭
C
F6
Repeat and Fade
yeah, yeah. Yeah, yeah, yeah.

DAYDREAM BELIEVER

Words and Music by
JOHN STEWART

2
F
Dm
Gm7
C7
F
shav - ing raz - or's cold and it stings.
Bb
C7
Am
Cheer up, sleep - y Jean.
Bb
C7
Dm
Bb
F
Oh, what can it mean to a day - dream be -
Bb
F
Dm
G7
liev - er and a home - com - ing queen.

C7
F
Gm
3fr
You once thought of me as a
good times start and end with - out
Am
B♭
1
F
white knight on a steed. Now you know how
dol - lar one to spend. But
Dm
G7
C7
hap - py I can be. Oh, and our
2
F
Dm
Gm7
C7
F
D.S. and Fade
how much, ba - by, do we real - ly need?

DO WAH DIDDY DIDDY

Words and Music by JEFF BARRY
and ELLIE GREENWICH

1
D7
fine. (Yeah, yeah) She looked good, she looked fine, and I near - ly lost my mind. Be -
door. (Yeah, yeah) We walked on to my door, and she
2
D7
G
Em
stayed a lit - tle more. My, my, my, my, I knew we were fall - in' in
more broadly
C
D7
love, My, my, my, my, I told her all the things I was
G
C
G
dream - in' of. Now we're to - geth - er near - ly ev - 'ry sin - gle day, sing - in'
3

C
G
do wah did - dy did - dy, down did - dy do; We're so hap - py and that's
C
G
how we're gon - na stay, sing - in' do wah did - dy did - dy, down
C
G
did - dy do.'Cause I'm
hers, (Yeah, yeah) and she's mine. (Yeah, yeah) Well, I'm hers and she's mine and the
G
wed - din' bells will chime, sing - in' do wah did - dy did - dy, down
C
G
Repeat and Fade
did - dy do.

DON'T BE CRUEL
(To a Heart That's True)

Words and Music by OTIS BLACKWELL
and ELVIS PRESLEY

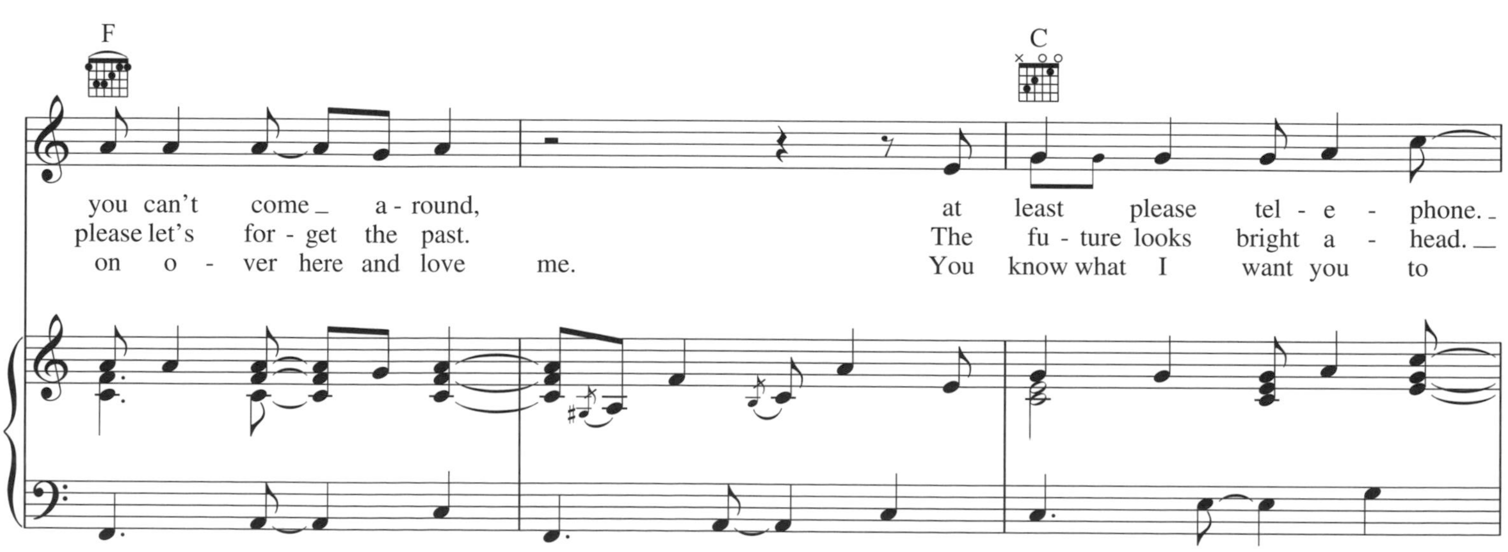

Dm
G
To Coda
Don't be cruel to a heart that's true.
Don't be cruel to a heart that's true.
say. Don't be cruel to a heart that's true.
C
1
2, 3
(2.) I don't
F
G
F
want no oth - er love.
Ba - by, it's just
Why should we be a - part,
I real - ly, real - ly love you,
G
C
1
D.S.
(take 2nd ending)
2, 3
N.C.
D.S. al Coda
you I'm think - in' of.
ba - by, cross my heart.

CODA
C
A
Solo ends
Let's
D
walk up to the preach - er.
Let us both say, "I do."
G
D
Then you'll know you have me and I know I'll have you, too.

Em7
A
Don't be cruel to a heart that's true.
D
Em/A
D
G
I don't want no oth - er love.
A
A♭
G
A
Ba - by, it's just you I'm think - in'
D
N.C.
Em7
of.
Don't be cruel

A
D
Em/A
D
to a heart that's true.
Don't you be cruel
Em7
A
D
Em/A
to a heart that's true.
D
Em7
A
'Said don't you be cruel
to a heart that's
D
Em/A
Repeat and Fade
D
Optional Ending
D
true.
No, don't be cruel

DREAM BABY
(How Long Must I Dream)

Words and Music by
CINDY WALKER

I'm dream - in' of you. That won't do.
A7
Dream ba - by, make me stop my dream - in'. You can make my dreams come
D
A7
true. Sweet dream
ba - by. Sweet

dream
ba - by,
D7
Sweet
dream
ba - by,
A7
how
long
must
I
1
D
dream?
2
D
dream?

DREAM LOVER

Words and Music by
BOBBY DARIN

C
G7
C
want a girl to call my
F
C
Am
Dm7
G7sus
G7
own. I want a dream lov - er so I don't have to dream a - lone.
C
G7
C
Dream lov - er,
Dream lov - er,
where are you,
un - til then,
Am
with a love, oh, so true,
I'll go to sleep and dream a - gain.

C
Am
and a hand that I can hold to feel you near when
That's the on - ly thing to do un - til my lov - er's
C
G7
I grow old?
dreams come true.
Be - cause I want a girl to
C
F
C
Am
call my own, I want a dream lov - er so
Dm7
G7sus
G7
To Coda
C
C7
I don't have to dream a - lone.

F
F7
C
Some - day, I don't know how, I hope you'll
hear my plea.
D7
Some way, I don't know how,
G7
D.S. al Coda
she'll bring her love to me.
CODA
C

EARTH ANGEL

Words and Music by
JESSE BELVIN

E♭ Cm Fm7 B♭7 E♭ Cm
an - gel, earth an - gel, the one I a - dore, love you for - ev - er and
Fm7 B♭7 E♭ Cm Fm7 B♭7
ev - er - more. I'm just a fool, a fool in love with
E♭ A♭ E♭ Fm7 E♭7 A♭ A♭m E♭
you. I fell for you, and I knew the
Fm7 B♭7 E♭ E♭7 A♭ Cdim
vi - sion of your love's love - li - ness. I hope and I pray

E♭
Cm
F9
B7
B♭7
3fr
that some - day I'll be the vi - sion of your hap - pi - ness. Earth
Fm7
an - gel, earth an - gel, please be mine; my dar - ling, dear,
love you all the time. I'm just a fool, a fool in love with
1
2
Cdim
E♭6/9
5fr
you. Earth
you.

GET A JOB

Words and Music by EARL BEAL, RICHARD LEWIS,
RAYMOND EDWARDS and WILLIAM HORTON

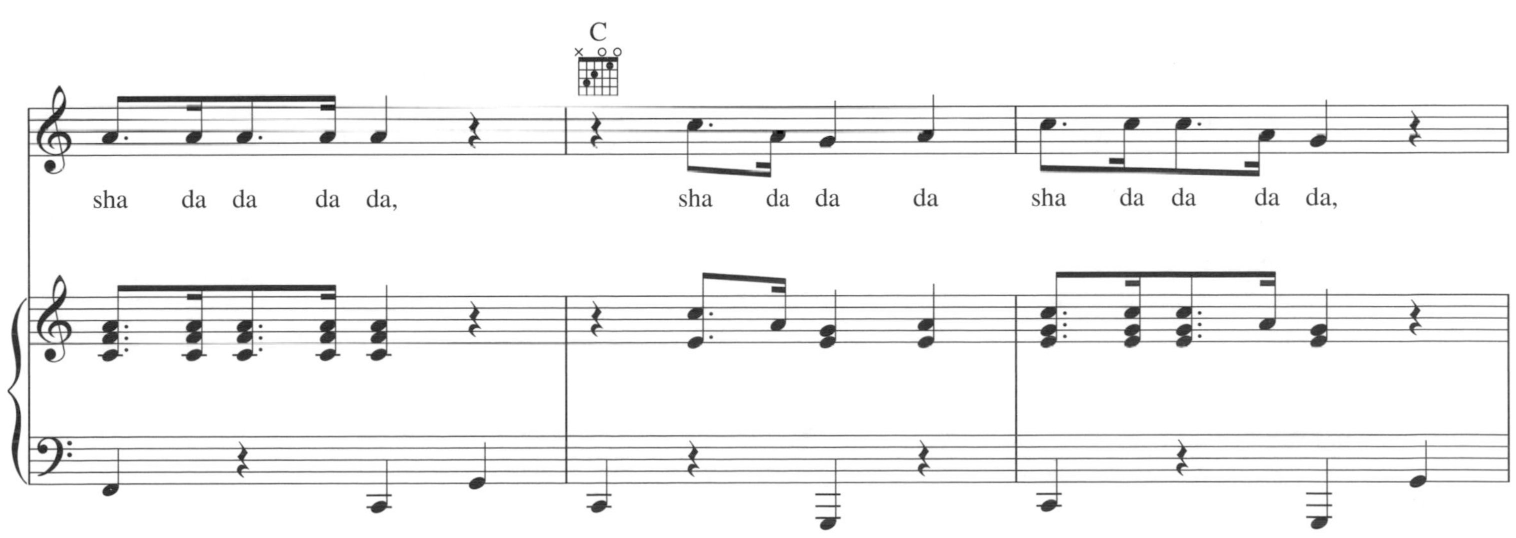

G7
F
G
C
To Coda
yip yip yip yip yip yip yip yip, mum mum mum mum mum mum. Get a job, sha da da da
Dm7
C
F
C
3
sha da da da da. Ev - 'ry morn - ing a - bout this time she get me out of my bed a - cry - ing get a
F
job. After break - fast ev - 'ry day, she throws the
G7
want ads right my way and nev - er fails to say, get a

C
job. Sha da da da sha da da da da, sha da da da
sha da da da da,
F
sha da da da sha da da da da,
C
sha da da da sha da da da da,
G7
yip yip yip yip yip yip yip yip,
F
mum mum mum mum mum mum. Get a
G
C
job, sha da da da sha da da da da, and

F
C
when I get the paper, I read it through and through and
D7
G7
my {girl / wife} nev-er fails to say if there is an-y work for me.
C
And when I go back to the house I
hear the wom-an's mouth preach-ing and a-cry-ing, tell me that I'm ly-ing 'bout a

G7
C
D.S. al Coda
job that I nev - er could find. Sha da da da
CODA
sha da da da da, sha da da da sha da da da da,
sha da da da sha da da da da, sha da da da
sha da da da da, sha da da da sha da da da da.

FUN, FUN, FUN

Words and Music by BRIAN WILSON
and MIKE LOVE

D
G
ra - di - o blast - in', goes cruis - in' just as fast as she can now.
guys try to catch her, but she leads 'em on a wild goose chase now.
D
F#m
G
A7
And she'll have fun, fun, fun, till her dad - dy takes the T - bird a - way.
D
G
1
D
A7
A7#5
2
D
A7
Well, the
D
G
D

A7
A7♯5
D
A - well, you knew all a - long that your
G
dad was get - tin' wise to you now.
And since he
D
took your set of keys you've been think - ing that your fun is all through
A7
now.
A7♯5
D
But you can come a - long with me, 'cause we

G
got - ta lot - ta things to do now.
And you'll have
D
F#m
G
A7
D
G
fun, fun, fun, now that dad - dy took the T - bird a - way.
1
D
A7#5
And you'll have
2
D
E7
A
And you'll have fun, fun, fun, now that
D
Repeat and Fade
G7
Optional Ending
dad - dy took the T - bird a - way.

GOOD GOLLY MISS MOLLY

Words and Music by ROBERT BLACKWELL
and JOHN MARASCALCO

F7
When you're rock - in' and a -
C7
Bb7
F7
roll - in', can't hear your mom-ma call.
C7#5
8fr
F
Bb7
F
Bb7
From the ear - ly, ear - ly morn-in' to the ear - ly, ear - ly night, when I
Mom-ma, Pop-pa told me, "Son, you'd bet-ter watch your step." If they
F
N.C.
F
N.C.
F
call, Miss Mol - ly's rock - in' at the House of Blue Lights. Good gol - ly Miss
knew a - bout Miss Mol - ly, have to watch my Pop my - self. Go - ing to the

B♭7
F7
Mol - ly, sure likes to ball.
cor - ner, gon - na buy a dia - mond ring.
C7
When you're rock - in' and a - roll - in',
When she hugs me and kiss - es me,
B♭7
1
F7
can't hear your mom - ma call.
makes me ting - a - ling - a -
C7♯5
8fr
2
F7
E♭
3fr
F
ling.

THE GREAT PRETENDER

Words and Music by
BUCK RAM

E♭ Fm/B♭ B♭7 E♭ E♭7 A♭
3fr 3fr 4fr
yes, I'm the great pre - tend - er, a - drift in a world of my
E♭ E♭7 A♭ B♭7 E♭ E♭/G A♭ Fm7
own. I play the game, but to my real shame, you've
E♭/B♭ Fm/B♭ B♭7 E♭ E♭7 A♭
6fr
left me to dream all a - lone. Too real is this feel - ing of
E♭ E♭7 A♭
make - be - lieve, too real when I feel what my

E♭/B♭ B♭7 E♭ Fm/B♭ B♭7 E♭ E♭7
heart can't con-ceal. Oh, yes, I'm the great pre-tend-er, just
A♭ E♭ E♭7 A♭ B♭7
laugh-in' and gay like a clown. I seem to be what I'm
E♭ E♭/G A♭ Fm7 E♭/B♭ Fm/A♭ G B♭7
not, you see; I'm wear-in' my heart like a crown, pre-
E♭ E♭/G Fm/A♭ B♭7
tend-in' that you're still a-roun'.
1
E♭ F7 Fm/B♭ B♭7
Oh,
2
E♭
roun'.

THE GREEN DOOR

Words and Music by BOB DAVIE
and MARVIN MOORE

D
A
There's an old pi - a - no and they play it hot _ be-hind the green door. _
Saw an eye - ball peep - ing through a smok - y cloud _ be-hind the green door. _
D
Don't know what they're do - ing but they laugh a lot _ be - hind the
When I said Joe sent _ me some-one laughed out loud _ be - hind the
A
E7
D7
green door. _ Wish they'd let me in _ so I could find out what's _ be-hind the
green door. _ All I want to do _ is join the hap - py crew _ be-hind the
1
A
green door. _
2
A
A13
5fr
green door. _

HAPPY TOGETHER

Words and Music by GARRY BONNER
and ALAN GORDON

2
B
geth - er.
E
Bm7
E
I can see me lov - in' no - bod - y but you for all my life.
G
E
Bm7
When you're with me, ba - by, the skies - 'll be
E
G
Em
blue for all my life.
Me and you, and you and

D
me, no mat - ter how they toss the dice, it had to be. The on - ly one for
C
To Coda
B
me is you, and you for me, so hap - py to - geth - er.
E
Bm7
Ba ba ba ba ba ba
Instrumental
E
G
E
ba ba ba ba ba. Ba ba ba ba

Bm7
E
Bm7
D.S. al Coda
(no repeats)
ba ba ba ba ba ba ba.
Instrumental ends
CODA
B
Em
B
geth - er, so hap - py to - geth - er.
Em
B
Em
B
Repeat ad lib.
And how is the weath - er? So hap - py to - geth - er.
Em
B
E
So hap - py to - geth - er.

HELLO MARY LOU

Words and Music by GENE PITNEY
and C. MANGIARACINA

B♭ B♭maj7 B♭6 B♭ E♭
I'm not one that gets a - round, I swear my feet stuck
thought a - bout a moon - lit night, my arms a - bout you
Edim7 B♭/F Gm E♭ F7♭9
to the ground, and though I nev - er did meet you be -
good an' tight; that's all I had to see for me to
B♭ F7
fore. I said, "Hel - lo, Mar - y
stay.
B♭ F7/C B♭7/D E♭ B♭
Lou, good - bye, heart. Sweet Mar - y Lou, I'm

C7
F7
so in love with you.
B♭
F7
B♭
D7
D+
D7
Gm
3fr
Knew, Mar - y Lou, we'd nev - er part, so hel -
C7
F7
1
B♭
lo, Mar - y Lou, good - bye, heart."
F7
2
B♭
I heart."

I GET AROUND

Words and Music by BRIAN WILSON
and MIKE LOVE

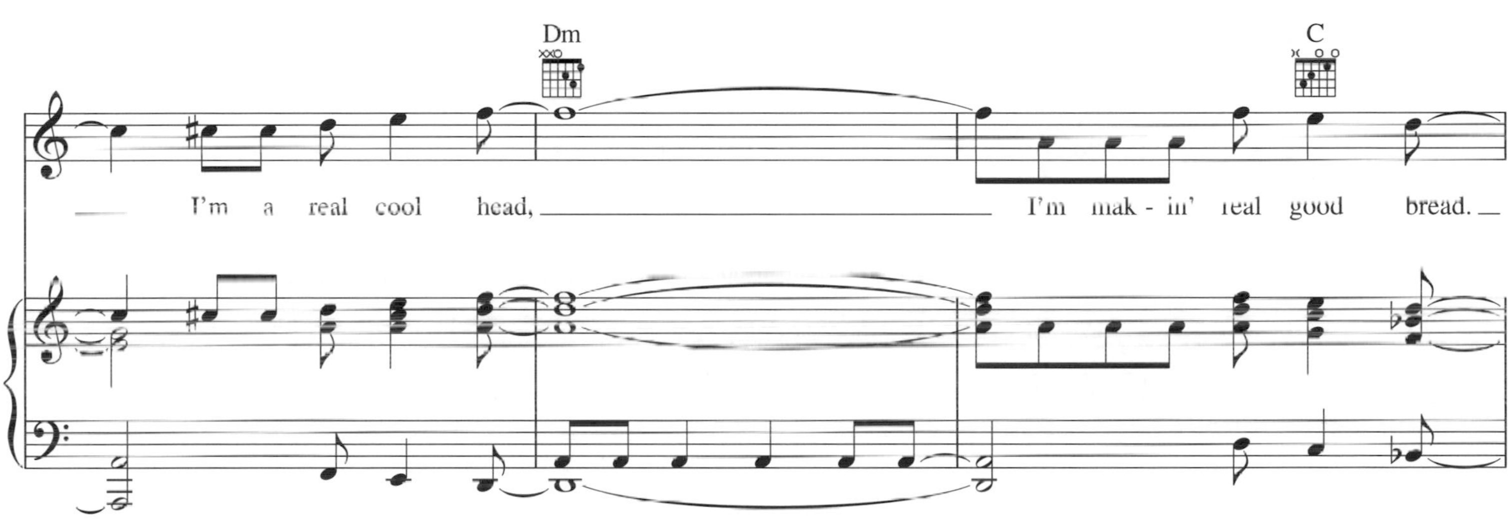

same ol' strip, I got - ta find a new place where the kids are hip.
nev - er been beat and we've nev - er missed yet with the girls we meet.
My bud - dies and me are get - tin'
None of the guys go stead - y 'cause it
real well - known, yeah, the bad guys know us and they leave us a - lone.
would - n't be right to leave your best girl home on a Sat - ur - day night.
I get a -
C
A7
round from town to town.

Dm
C
B♭
I'm a real cool head, I'm mak-in' real good bread.
1
G7
2
G7
C
We I get a-round from town to
A7
Dm
town. I'm a real cool head,
C
B♭
G7
Repeat and Fade
Optional Ending
C
I'm mak-in' real good bread. I get a-round.

HEY PAULA

Words and Music by
RAY HILDEBRAND

G
Am7
G
D7
G
Em
love, my love. She: Hey! Paul, I've been
3
Am7
D7
G
Em7
Am7
D7
wait - ing for you. Hey! Hey! Hey! Paul, I wan - na mar - ry you, too, if
G
Em
G
Em7
Am7
you love me true, if you love me still. Our love will al - ways be
Am7/D
5fr
D7
G
Am7
G
D7
real, my love, my love.
3
3

G
Em7
Am7
D7
Am7
D7
Both: True love means plan - ning a life for two, be - ing to - geth - er the
G
E7
Am
whole day through. True love means wait - ing and hop - ing that soon
A7
Am7/D
5fr
D7
G
Am7
wish - es we've made will come true, my love, my
G
D7
G
Em7
Am7
D7
love. He: Hey! Hey! Paul - a, I've been wait - ing for you. She: Hey! Hey!

G Em7 Am7 D7 G Em7
Paul, I want to mar - ry you, _ too. Both: True love means plan - ning a
Am7 D7 Am7 D7 G
life for two, be - ing to - geth - er the whole day through.
E7 Am A7
True love means wait - ing and hop - ing that soon wish - es we've made _ will come
Am7/D 5fr D7 G Am7 G A♭9♯11 G6/9
true, my _ love, my _ love.
molto rit.

HUSHABYE

Words and Music by DOC POMUS
and MORT SHUMAN

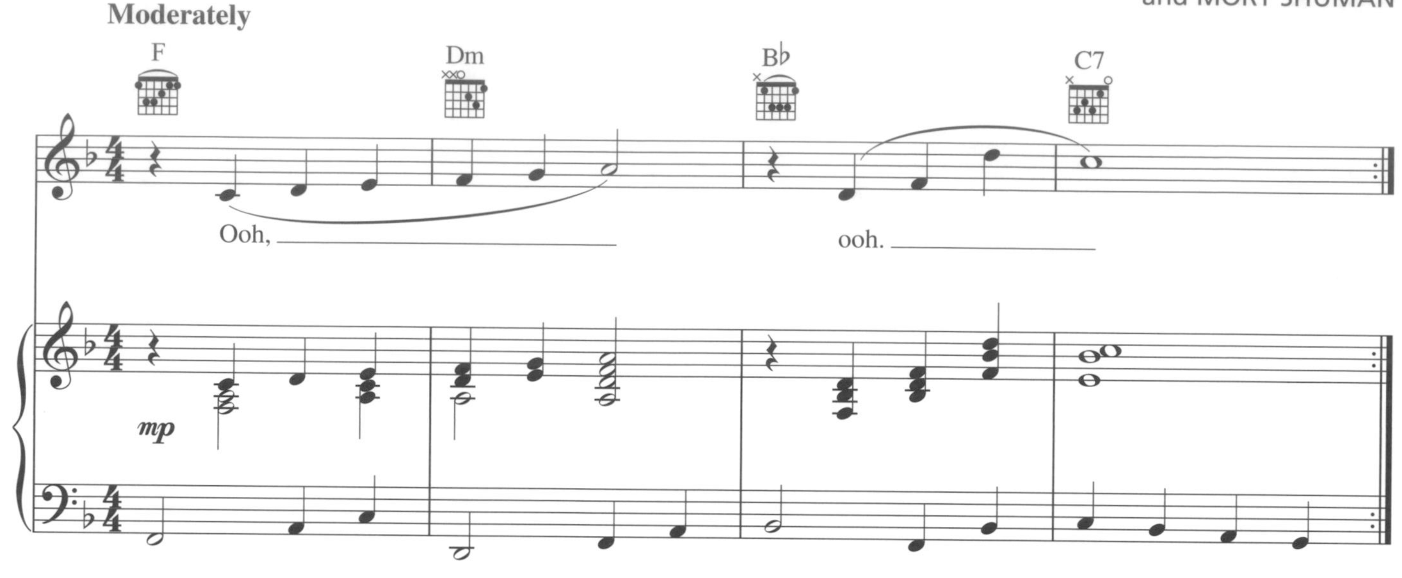

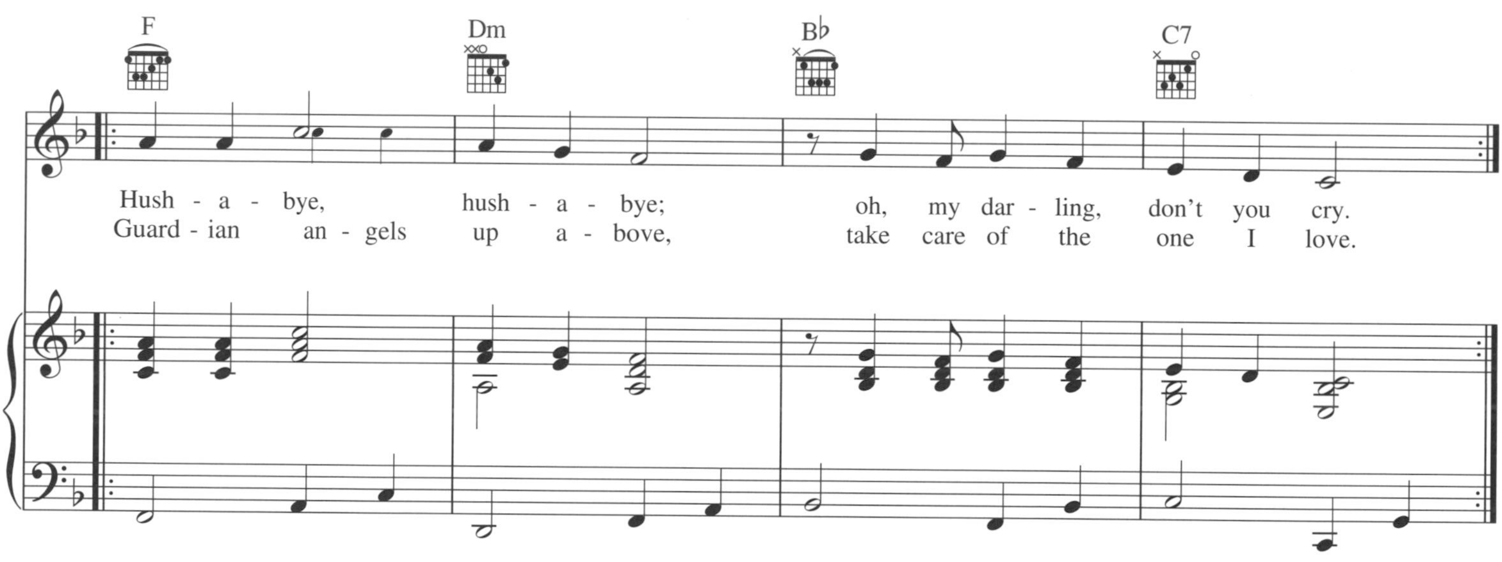

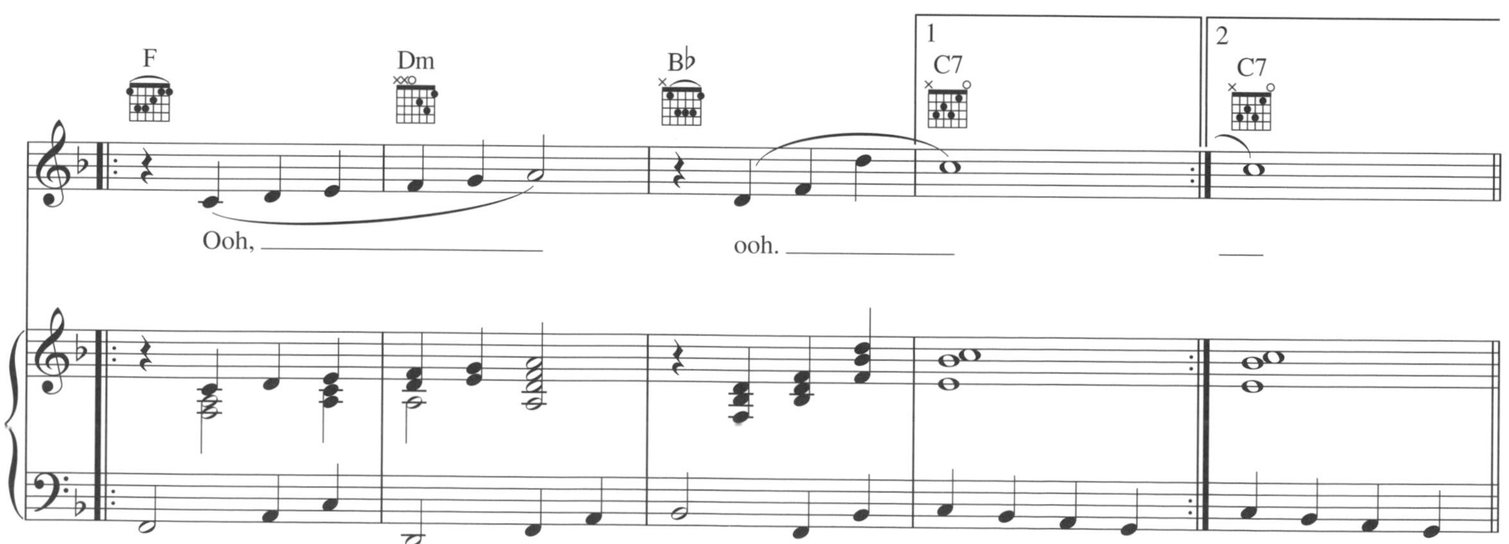

F
Dm
B♭
C7
Hush - a - bye, hush - a - bye; oh, my dar - ling, don't you cry.
Guard - ian an - gels up a - bove, take care of the one I love.
Ooh, ooh.
Pil - lows ly - ing on your bed; oh, my dar - ling, rest your head.
Sand - man will be com - ing soon, sing - ing you a slum - ber tune.
Ooh, ooh.

F
B♭
F
F7
Ooh.
Lull - a -
B♭
F
by
and good - night.
In your
C7
F
F7
dreams
I'll hold you tight.
Lull - a -
B♭
F
by
and good - night
till the

C7
F
dawn's
ear - ly
light.
F
Dm
B♭
C7
Hush - a - bye,
hush - a - bye;
oh, my dar - ling,
don't you cry.
Guard - ian
an - gels,
up a - bove,
take care of the
one I love.
F
Dm
B♭
1
C7
Ooh,
ooh.
2
C7
F
B♭
F

('Til) I KISSED YOU

Words and Music by
DON EVERLY

F
C7
Nev - er had you on my mind; now you're there all the time.
Mmm, you got a way a - bout you; now I can't live with-out you.
F
Dm
F
Dm
Nev - er knew what I missed un - til I kissed you.
Uh huh, I
1
F
Dm
2
F
Dm
kissed you,
oh yeah.
kissed you,
oh yeah.
Dm
F
You don't re - al - ize what you do to me.
And
f

Dm
F
I didn't re - al - ize what a kiss could be.
F
C7
Mmm, you got a way a - bout you; now I can't live with-out you.
F
Dm
F
Dm
Nev - er knew what I missed un - til I kissed you. Uh huh, I
F
Dm
F
kissed you, oh yeah, I kissed you.

I WANT YOU, I NEED YOU, I LOVE YOU

Words by MAURICE MYSELS
Music by IRA KOSLOFF

C Am Dm G7 C C7
time that you're near all my cares dis - ap - pear. Darling, you're all that I'm liv-ing
F C E7 A7
for. I want you, I need you, I love you
Dm7 G7 C Fm C Gm7 C7
more and more. I thought I could live with-out
F Gm7 C7sus C7 F
ro - mance, be - fore you came to me. But

Am7
D7
G
Em
Am7
D7
now I know that I will go on lov - ing you e - ter - nal -
G7sus
G7
C
Am
Dm
G7
ly. Won't you please be my own? Nev - er leave me a - lone, 'cause I
C
C7
F
C
E7
die ev - 'ry time we're a - part. I want you, I need you, I
A7
Dm7
G7
C
A♭7
G7
C
love you with all my heart. Hold me heart.

IN MY ROOM

Words and Music by BRIAN WILSON
and GARY USHER

1 C
B♭
C
room.
(In my room.)
2 C
B♭
C
room.
(In my room.)
Am
G
Do my dream - ing and my schem - ing,
Am G Am G C
Am
lie a - wake and pray.
Do my cry - ing

G
Dm7
and my sigh - ing, laugh at yes - ter -
G7
D.S. al Coda
day.
CODA
C
B♭
room.
(In my
C
B♭
C
B♭
Room.
room, in my room, in my
C
B♭
C
B♭
C
room, in my room, in my room.)

JAILHOUSE ROCK

Words and Music by JERRY LEIBER
and MIKE STOLLER

D7
E♭7
Chorus
gan to swing. You should have heard those knocked - out jail - birds sing. Let's
A♭7
E♭7
rock! Ev - 'ry - bod - y let's rock!
To Coda
B♭7
A♭7
Ev - 'ry - bod - y in the whole cell block was danc -
1-3
E♭7
D7
4
E♭7
- ing to the Jail - house Rock!
- ing to the Jail - house

Additional Lyrics

2. Spider Murphy played the tenor saxophone
   Little Joe was blowin' on the slide trombone.
   The drummer boy from Illinois went crash, boom, bang;
   The whole rhythm section was the Purple Gang.
   Chorus

3. Number forty-seven said to number three
   "You're the cutest jailbird I ever did see.
   I sure would be delighted with your company,
   Come on and do the Jailhouse Rock with me."
   Chorus

4. The sad sack was a-sittin' on a block of stone,
   Way over in the corner weeping all alone.
   The warden said: "Hey, Buddy, don't you be no square,
   If you can't find a partner, use a wooden chair!"
   Chorus

5. Shifty Henry said to Bugs: "For heaven's sake,
   No one's lookin', now's our chance to make a break."
   Bugsy turned to Shifty and he said: "Nix, nix;
   I wanna stick around a while and get my kicks."
   Chorus

IT'S MY PARTY

Words and Music by HERB WIENER,
WALLY GOLD and JOHN GLUCK, JR.

C
D7
G7
holding her hand, when he's supposed to be mine?
dancing with me, I've got no reason to smile.
birthday surprise; Judy's wearing his ring.
C
C+
F
It's my party, and I'll cry if I want to, cry if I want to,
Fm
C
G7
cry if I want to. You would cry, too, if it happened to
C
F
C
1, 2
G7
3
G7
C
you.

IT'S ONLY MAKE BELIEVE

Words and Music by CONWAY TWITTY
and JACK NANCE

C
Am
My one and on - ly prayer, is that some - day you'll care,
F
G7
my hopes, my dreams come true, my one and on - ly you,
F
G
no one will ev - er know, how much I love you so.
C
F
My on - ly prayer will be, some - day you'll care for me, but it's

G
F6
C
F
on - ly make be - lieve.
C
A7
D
My hopes, my dreams come true,
My one and on - ly prayer
Bm
my life I'd give for you,
is that some - day you'll care,
G
my heart a wed - ding ring,
my hopes, my dreams come true,
A7
my all, my ev - 'ry - thing.
my one and on - ly you.
G
My heart I can't con - trol,
No one will ev - er know,

A
D
you rule my ver - y soul, my plans, my hopes, my schemes,
just how much I love you so, my on - ly prayer will be
G
A
you are my ev - 'ry - thing, but it's on - ly make
that some - day you'll care for me but it's on - ly make
G
D
G
D
A7
be - lieve.
be -
D
G
D
G
D
lieve.

IT'S SO EASY

Words and Music by BUDDY HOLLY
and NORMAN PETTY

B♭7
E♭
3fr
C7
(Hum) it seems so eas - y. Where you're con - cerned my
F7
B♭
F9
E♭
F7
B♭
E♭
To Coda
heart has learned: It's so eas - y to fall in love. It's so eas - y to
mf
F7
E♭/F
B♭
F9
E♭
F7
B♭
E♭
fall in love! Look in - to your heart and see what your love book has
D.S. al Coda
F7
B♭
B♭7
set a - part for me. It seems so
3
f
CODA
F7
E♭/F
B♭
fall in love!

KANSAS CITY

Words and Music by JERRY LEIBER
and MIKE STOLLER

G7
F7
cra - zy way of lov - in' there and I'm gon - na get me some.
C7
I'm gon - na be
C
stand - in' on the cor - ner
pack my clothes,
Twelfth Street and Vine.
leave at the crack of dawn.
I'm gon - na be
I'm go - in' to

F7
stand - in' on the cor - ner ___ Twelfth Street and Vine, ___
pack ___ my clothes, ___ leave at the ___ crack of dawn. ___
C
with my
My old
G7
F7
Kan - sas Cit - y ba - by and a bot - tle of Kan - sas ___ Cit - y wine. ___
la - dy will be sleep - in' an' she won't ___ know ___ where I'm gone. ___
3
C7
Well, ___ I
'Cause if I

C
F7
might take a train, I might take a plane, but
stay with that wom - an I know I'm gon - na die, got - ta
C
if I have to walk I'm goin' just the same. I'm go - in' to
find a brand - new ba - by and that's the rea - son why I'm go - in' to
F7
Kan - sas Cit - y, Kan - sas Cit - y here I
C
come. They got a

G7
F7
cra - zy way of lov - in' there and I'm gon - na get me some.
C7
1
I'm go - in' to
2
They got a cra - zy way of lov - in' there and
G7
F7
C7
I'm gon - na get me some.

LA BAMBA

By RITCHIE VALENS

C
F
G7
ba;
ar - ri - ba ar - ri - ba por tí se re
por tí se re se re.
Yo no soy mar - i -
ne - ro.
Yo no soy mar - i - ne - ro, soy cap - i - tán;
yo no soy mar - i - ne - ro, soy cap - i - tán.
To Coda

C
F
G7
Bam - ba bam - ba, bam - ba bam -
- ba, bam - ba bam - ba,
N.C.
D.S. al Coda
bam - ba bam... Pa - ra bai - lar la bam -
CODA
Repeat and Fade
Optional Ending
Bam - ba bam - ba!

LIMBO ROCK

Words and Music by BILLY STRANGE
and JON SHELDON

Moderately slow Calypso

E♭
A♭
do the lim - bo rock all a - round the lim - bo block.
an - kle, lim - bo knee, bend back like a lim - bo tree. Jack be
lim - bo moon - a - bove, you will fall in lim - bo love.
D♭
A♭
E♭
lim - ber, Jack be quick, Jack go un - der lim - bo stick. All a -
To Coda
1
A♭
D♭
A♭
N.C.
round the lim - bo clock, hey let's do the lim - bo rock.
(Spoken:) Limbo lower now,
limbo
Percussion:

lower now.
How low can you go?
First, you
2
A♭
D♭
A♭
4fr
do the lim - bo rock.
La, la, la, la, la, la, la, la; la, la, la,
E♭
3fr
A♭
4fr
la, la, la, la, la; la, la, la, la, la, la, la, la; la, la, la,
E♭
3fr
A♭
4fr
D♭
la, la, la, la, la; la, la, la, la, la, la, la, la; la, la, la,

A♭
E♭
la, la, la, __ la, la; la, la, la, la, la, la, __ la, la; la, la, la,
A♭
D♭
A♭
D.S. al Coda
la, la, la, __ la, la. Get your -
CODA
A♭
D♭
A♭
N.C.
do the lim - bo rock.
(Spoken:) Don't move that limbo bar. You'll be a limbo star.
Percussion:
How low can you go?
La, la, la,

A♭ 4fr
E♭ 3fr
A♭ 4fr
la, la, la, la, la; la, la, la, la, la, la, la, la; la, la, la,
E♭ 3fr
A♭ 4fr
la, la, la, la, la; la, la, la, la, la, la, la, la; la, la, la,
D♭
A♭ 4fr
E♭ 3fr
la, la, la, la, la; la, la, la, la, la, la, la, la; la, la, la,
A♭ 4fr
D♭
A♭ 4fr
la, la, la, la, la; la, la, la, la, la, la, la, la.

LITTLE DARLIN'

Words and Music by
MAURICE WILLIAMS

Gm
3fr
I was wrong
to
3
Cm7
3fr
F7
try
to love _ two,
B♭6
know - ing well
that my
Gm
3fr
Cm7
3fr
love
was _ just
3

(Spoken over repeat:) (optional)
My dear, I need your love to call my own
And never do wrong; and to hold in mine your little hand.
I'll know too soon that I'll love again.
Please come back to me.

LONELY BOY

Words and Music by
PAUL ANKA

Bm7
A
Em
thing you could think of, but all I
A
Em7
A
A7
D
C
D
Fine
want is some-one to love.
Some-one, yes, some-one to
Bm7
A
A7
Em
love, some-one to kiss.
Some-one to
A
Em7
A7
D
hold at a mo-ment like this.
I'd like to

Bm7 A Em
hear some-bod - y say, "I'll give you my
A A7 D C D A7
love each night and day." A life-time of love means
D A7 D D7
more to me than rich - es or fame un - told.
G D E9
Some-where there's a some-one wait-ing for me. I'll find her be-fore I grow too

A7
D
Bm7
old. Some-bod - y, some-bod - y, some-bod - y, please send her to
A
A7
Em
A
Em7
A7
me. I'll make her hap - py, just wait and
D
Em
see. I prayed so hard to the heav-ens a -
A
Em
A
A7
D
Am7
D
D.S. al Fine
bove that I might find some-one to love. I'm just a

LONELY TEARDROPS

Words and Music by BERRY GORDY,
GWEN GORDY FUQUA and TYRAN CARLO

F7
N.C.
home, come home. Just say you
B♭
will, say you will, say you
Gm
E♭
will. Hey hey.
B♭
Cm7
B♭
E♭
My heart is cry - in', cry - in'. Lone - ly tear - drops,

E♭m
6fr
B♭
my pil - low's nev - er dry.
Lone - ly
tear - drops,
come
home,
come
F7
home.
N.C.
Just say you will,
say you
B♭
will,
say you
Gm
3fr
will.
Hey

E♭
3fr
B♭
hey.
Just
B♭9
B♭7
E♭
3fr
give me an - oth - er chance for
E♭m
6fr
B♭
our ro - mance, come on and tell me
3
3
D7
that one day you'll re - turn, 'cause
3
3
3

Eb
3fr
Ebm
6fr
ev - 'ry day that you've been gone a -
F7
Bb
way, you'll know how my heart does noth - ing but burn.
Bb
Eb
3fr
Cry - in' lone - ly tear-drops, my pil - low's
Ebm
6fr
Bb
nev-er dry. Lone - ly tear-drops, come

F7
N.C.
home, come home.
Just say you
B♭
will, say you will,
say you
Gm
3fr
B♭
will.
Hey hey,
say it right now,
Gm
3fr
B♭
ba - by.
Come on, come on.

LONESOME TOWN

Words and Music by
BAKER KNIGHT

C
E7
F
G9
9fr
3
stay. (Lone-some Town.) You can buy a dream or two _ to last you all through the
C
F
Fm
C
Am
Dm7
G7
years. And the on - ly price you pay is a heart full of
C
F
Em
tears. (Full of tears.) Go - in' down to Lone - some Town, _
mf
Dm7
G7
C
F
Em
where the bro - ken hearts stay; go - in' down to Lone - some Town, _ to

D7
G7
C
E7
cry my trou-bles a - way.
In the town of bro - ken dreams the
rall.
mp a tempo
F
G9
9fr
C
F
Fm
C
Am
streets are paved with re - gret;
may-be down in Lone - some Town
Dm7
G7
C
F
Fm
C
Am
I can learn to for - get. (To for- get.)
may-be down in Lone - some Town
Dm7
G7
C
Fm/C
C
I can learn to for - get.
(Lone - some Town.)
rit.

MY BOY LOLLIPOP

Words and Music by MORRIS LEVY
and JOHNNY ROBERTS

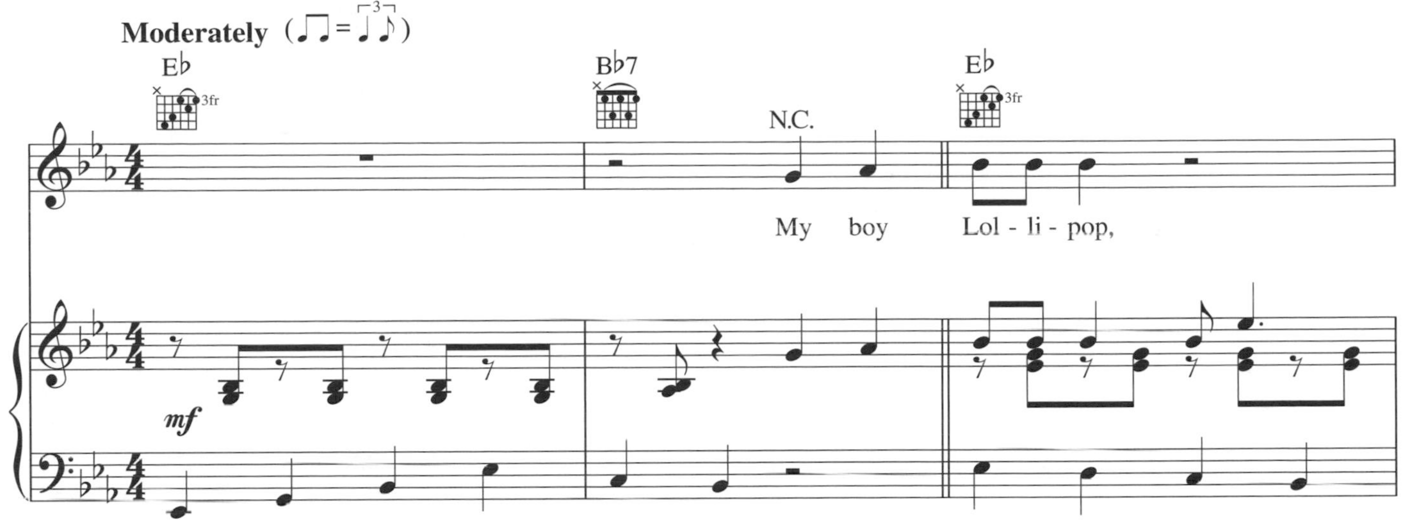

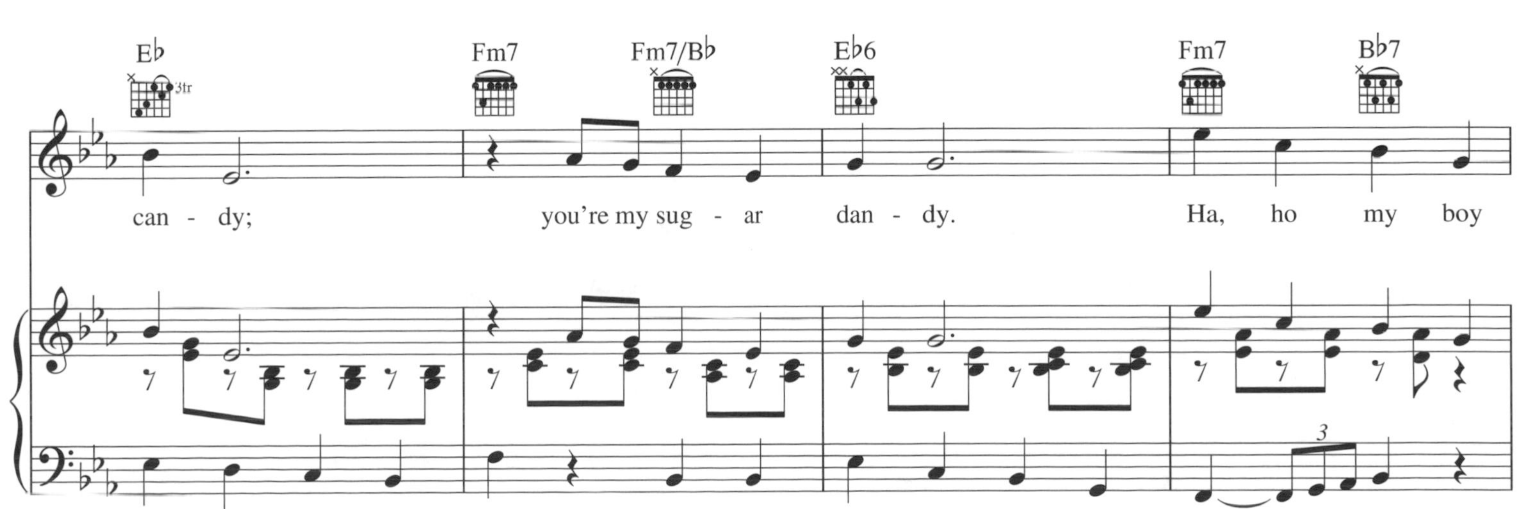

E♭
A♭6
E♭
Lol - li - pop,
nev - er ev - er leave me,
A♭6
E♭
Fm7
B♭7
be-cause it would grieve me;
my heart told me
E♭
E♭7
A♭
so.
I love ya, I love ya, I love ya so;
E♭
E♭7
A♭
that I want you to know.
I need ya, I need ya, I need ya so, and

B♭
N.C.
B♭7
E♭
A♭6
I'll nev-er let you go. My boy Lol-li-pop, you made my heart go
gid-dy up. You set my world on fire;
you are my one de - sire.
B♭6/F
Fm7
E♭/B♭
B♭7
My boy Lol - li -
pop!
Repeat and Fade
Optional Ending
My boy Lol - li - pop!

LOUIE, LOUIE

Words and Music by
RICHARD BERRY

* Lyrics omitted at the request of the publisher.

A
D
Em
D
A
D
Em
D
A
D
Em
D
1, 2
A
D
Em
D
3
A
D
Em
D
D.S. al Coda
CODA
A
D
Em
D
A
D
Em
D
A
D
Em
D
A

NO PARTICULAR PLACE TO GO

Words and Music by
CHUCK BERRY

F
C7
wild.
ear.
stroll.
budge.
Cruis-ing and play-ing the ra - di - o,
Cud - dling more and driv-ing slow,
Can you i - mag-ine the way I felt?
Cruis-ing and play-ing the ra - di - o,

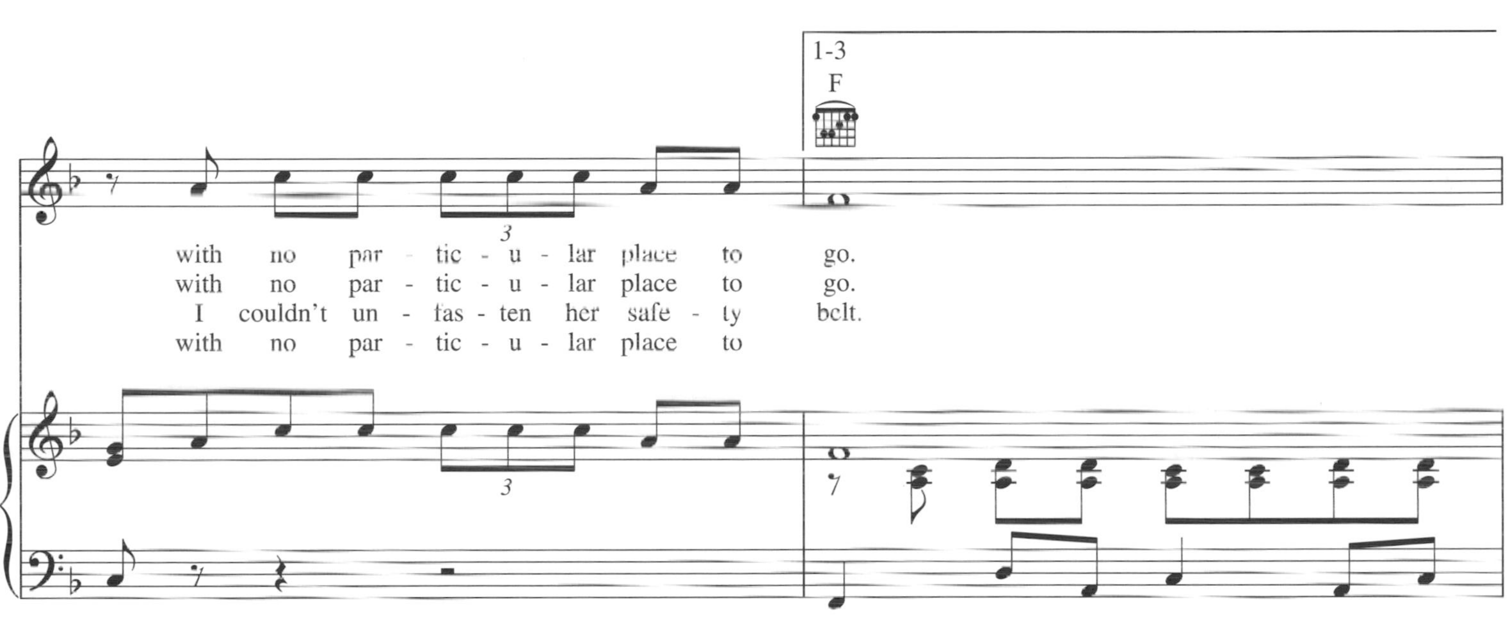
1-3
F
with no par - tic - u - lar place to go.
with no par - tic - u - lar place to go.
I couldn't un - fas - ten her safe - ty belt.
with no par - tic - u - lar place to

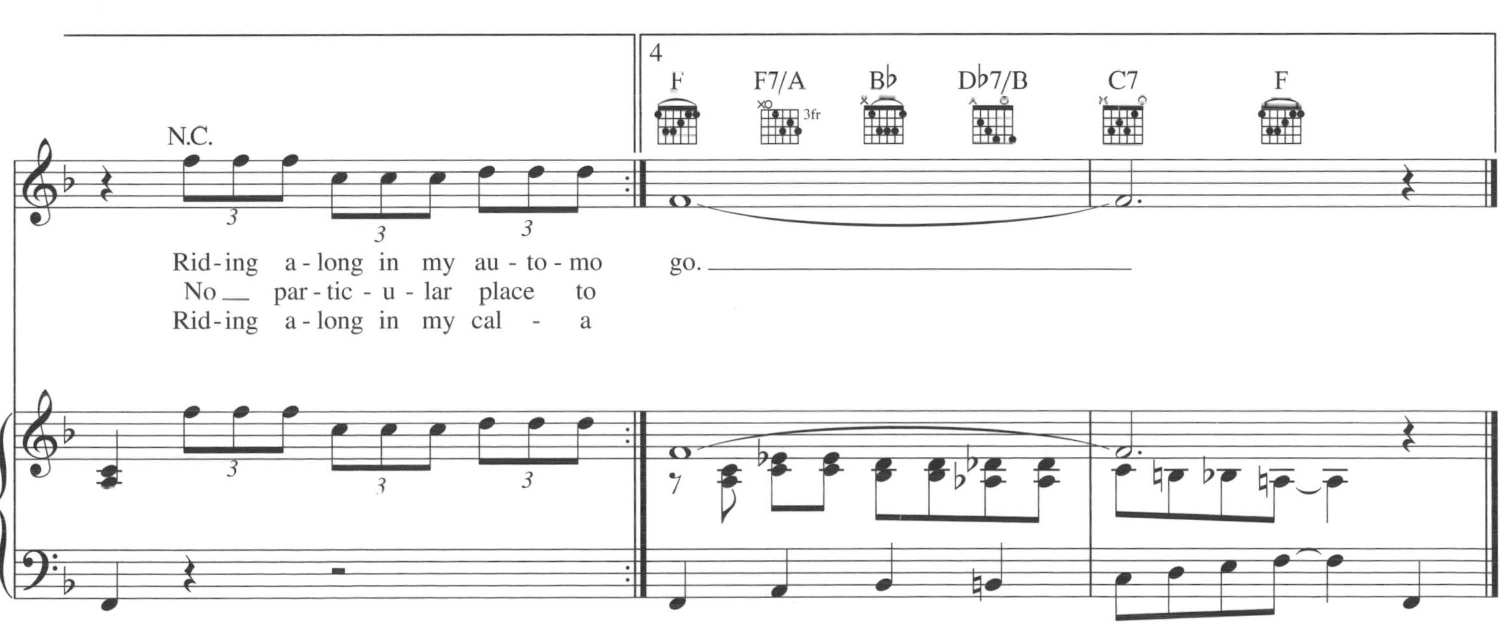
N.C.
4
F F7/A B♭ D♭7/B C7 F
Rid-ing a-long in my au-to-mo go.
No par-tic-u-lar place to
Rid-ing a-long in my cal - a

ONLY THE LONELY
(Know the Way I Feel)

Words and Music by ROY ORBISON
and JOE MELSON

G7
C
heart. They've gone for - ev - er, so far a -
mance, no more sor - row but that's the
A7
D7
G
G7
part. But on - ly the lone - ly know
chance. You've got to take if you're lone -
C
D7
why I cry, on - ly the
ly. Heart - break,
1
G
D7
2
G
lone - ly. On - ly the lone - ly.

PARTY DOLL

Words and Music by JAMES BOWEN
and BUDDY KNOX

G6
D7
Come a - long and be my par - ty doll.
Come a - long and be my
G6
C
par - ty doll.
Come a - long and be my par - ty doll.
D7
G6
To Coda
1
D7
I'll make love to you, to you,
I'll make love to you.
G6
2
D7
G6
Well, I'll make love to you.

G C G D7
Ev - 'ry man has got - ta have a par - ty doll, to be with him, when he's
G G7/B C
feel - in' wild; to be ev - er lov - in', true and fair; to
D7 G D7
run her fin - gers through his hair; to run her fin - gers
G
through his hair.
D.S. al Coda
CODA
D7 G6
I'll make love to you.

PEPPERMINT TWIST

Words and Music by JOSEPH DiNICOLA
and HENRY GLOVER

F9
C
the Pep - per - mint Twist.
C
'Round and 'round, up and down,
F9
C
'round and 'round, up and down, it's
To Coda
G9
3fr
F9
C
'round and 'round and up and down, one - two - three kick, one - two - three jump!

Meet me, ba - by, on For - ty - fifth Street
F9
C
where the Pep - per - mint Twist - ers meet.
You'll
G9
3fr
F9
C
learn to do this, the Pep - per - mint Twist.
D.S. al Coda
CODA
C
one - two - three kick, one - two - three jump!

PEGGY SUE

Words and Music by JERRY ALLISON,
NORMAN PETTY and BUDDY HOLLY

C
G
Oh, well, I
D7
C
C7
love you, gal, yes, I love you, Peg - gy Sue.
G
C
G
D7
G
Peg - gy Sue,
Peg - gy Sue,

E♭
3fr
G
pret - ty, pret - ty, pret - ty, pret - ty Peg - gy Sue, oh, my
C
Peg - gy, my Peg - gy Sue;
G
C
G
Oh, well, I
D7
C
C7
G
love you, gal, and I need you, Peg - gy Sue.

C
G
D7
G
C
I love you,
Peg - gy Sue,
G
C
G
D7
G7
with a love so rare and true,
oh,
C
G7
Peg - gy,
my Peg - gy Sue;

C
G
Oh, well, I
D7
love you, gal, yes, I want you, Peg - gy Sue.
1
D.S.
(with repeat)
2
G7

(You've Got) PERSONALITY

Words and Music by LLOYD PRINCE and HAROLD LOGAN

C7
F
F♯dim7
o - ver, my friends say I'm a fool. But
o - ver, they still say I'm a fool. But
C
B♭7
A7
D9
4fr
G7
o - ver and o - ver, I'll be a fool for
o - ver and o - ver, I'll be a fool for
C
N.C.
G7
you. 'Cause you've got per - son - al - i - ty, walk, a - per - son - al - i - ty, talk,
you.
C
G7
a - per - son - al - i - ty, smile, a - per - son - al - i - ty, charm, a - per - son - al - i - ty, love

C
F9
C7
a - per - son - al - i - ty, and 'course you've got a great big heart. So,
F
F♯dim7
C
B♭7♭5
5fr
o - ver and o - ver, oh, I'll be a fool for you.
A7
D7
G7
Now, o - ver and o - ver,
C
F6
1
C
G7♯5
2
C
C6
what more can I do?
do?

PLEASE MR. POSTMAN

Words and Music by ROBERT BATEMAN,
GEORGIA DOBBINS, WILLIAM GARRETT,
FREDDIE GORMAN and BRIAN HOLLAND

A
N.C.
might - y long time)
(since I heard from this boy-friend of mine.)
man.
Whoa, _
yeah. _
D
Bm
There must be some word to - day
from my boy-friend so
far a - way.
G
Please, Mis - ter Post - man, look and see;
A
N.C.
D
is there a let - ter, a let - ter for me?
I've been stand-ing here

Bm
wait - ing, Mis - ter Post - man, so, so pa - tient - ly
G
A
for just a card or just a let - ter say - ing he's re - turn - ing
N.C.
D
(Please, Mis - ter Post-man, look and see;)
home to me. Please, Mis - ter Post - man. Oh, yeah.
Bm
G
(is there a let - ter in your bag for me?) ('Cause it's been a
Please, please, Mis - ter Post -

A
N.C.
might - y long time)
man.
Whoa, __
yeah. _
(since I heard
from this
boy-friend of mine.)
D
Bm
So man - y days __ you've passed me by; ________
you saw the tears stand - ing
G
in my __ eyes. _____
You would - n't stop
to make me feel bet - ter
A
N.C.
D
by leav - ing me
a card or a let - ter.
Please, Mis - ter Post - man,

Bm
look and see; is there a let-ter, oh, yeah, in your bag for me? You know, it's
G
A
been so long, yeah, since I heard from this boy-friend
N.C.
D
of mine. You'd bet-ter wait a min-ute, wait a min-ute. Oh, you'd bet-ter
(Wait.) (Wait a min-ute, Mis-ter Post-man.)
Bm
G
wait a min-ute. Please, please, Mis-ter Post-man,
(Wait.) (Wait a min-ute, Mis-ter Post-man.) (Wait.) (Wait a

A
min - ute, Mis - ter Post - man.)
please check and __ see __ just one more time for me. __ You'd bet - ter
D
Bm
(Wait.) (Wait a min - ute, Mis - ter Post - man) (Wait. Wait a
wait. Wait a min - ute. Wait __ a min - ute, wait a min - ute, wait a min - ute.
G
min - ute, Mis - ter Post - man.) (Wait.) (Wait a min - ute, Mis - ter Post - man.)
Please, ___ Mis - ter Post - man. De -
Repeat ad lib. and Fade
Optional Ending
A
N.C.
D
liv - er de let - ter, the soon - er de bet - ter.

A ROSE AND A BABY RUTH

Words and Music by
JOHN D. LOUDERMILK

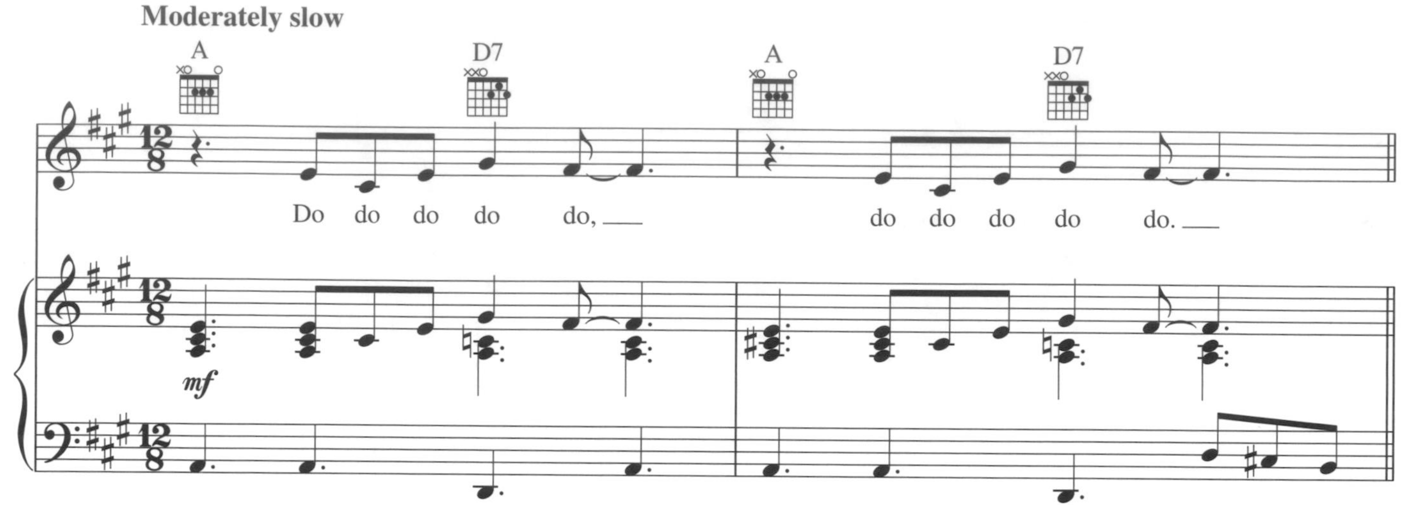

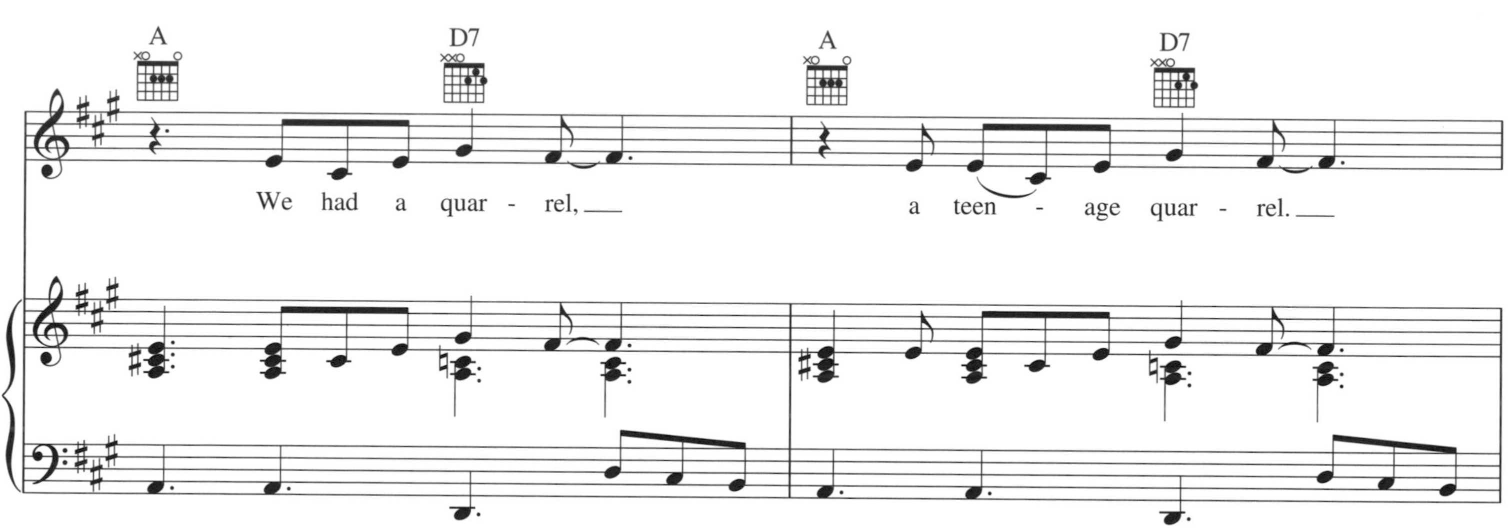

D7
Dm
A
F#7
I can't call you on the phone.
B7
E7
I can't e - ven see you at your home.
A
D7
A
D7
So, I'm send - ing you this pres - ent
But when we grow up, some - day I'll show up,
A
A7
just to prove that I'm tell - ing the truth.
just to prove I was tell - ing the truth.

D7
Dm
A
F#7
B7
E7
Dear, I be - lieve you won't laugh when you re-ceive
I'll kiss you, too, then I'll hand _ to you
this rose and ___ a Ba - by
Ruth. ______
Do do do do do, __
do do do do do. __
To Coda
A7
D
Ah. ______
I could have sent you ___ an or - chid of some kind,
2
but that's all I had in ___ my jeans ___ at the time.
D.S. al Coda
CODA
Ooh. ______

RUBY BABY

Words and Music by JERRY LEIBER
and MIKE STOLLER

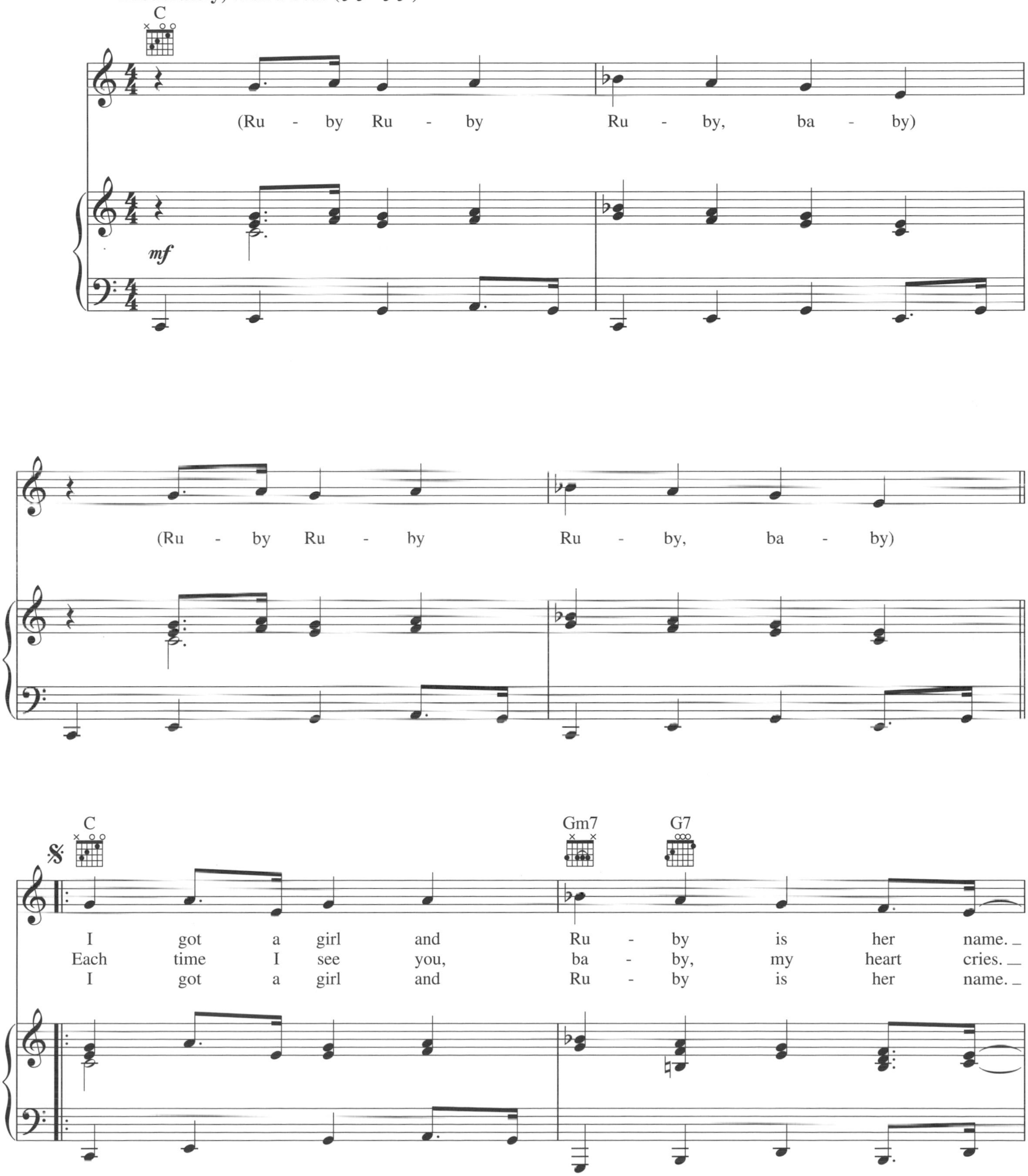

(Ru - by Ru - by Ru - by, ba - by)

C Gm7 G7

I got a girl and Ru - by is her name.
Each time I see you, ba - by, my heart cries.
I got a girl and Ru - by is her name.

C
(Ru - by Ru - by Ru - by, ba - by)
She
Gm7
G7
don't love me but I love her just the same.
I'm gon - na steal you a - way from all those guys.
I'd give the world just to set her heart a - flame.
C
(Ru - by Ru - by Ru - by ba - by)
F
Ru - by, Ru - by, how I want ya.
From the ver - y day I met ya,
Got some love 'n' mon - ey, too,

C
Like a ghost I'm gon - na haunt ya.
made a bet that I would get ya.
gon - na give it all to you.
G
F
C
To Coda
Ru - by, Ru - by when will you be mine? (Ru - by Ru - by
1
2
D.S. al Coda
Ru - by, ba - by) Ru - by, ba - by)
CODA
C
Ru - by, ba - by)
G
F
C
Repeat and Fade
Ru - by, Ru - by, when will you be mine? (Ru - by ba - by

RUNAWAY

Words and Music by DEL SHANNON
and MAX CROOK

C7
Fm
strong.
And as I
Eb
3fr
still walk on, I think of the things we've done to -
Db
C7
geth - er while our hearts were young.
F
I'm a - walk - in' in the rain.

Dm
Tears are fall - in' and I feel a pain,
F
a - wish - in' you were
here by me
Dm
to end this mis - er - y. And I
F
won - der,
wo - wo - wo - wo -
Dm
won - der
F
why,
why why why why

Dm
F
why she ran a - way and I wonder
where she will stay,
C7
B♭/C
my lit - tle
F
B♭
1
run - a - way,
run - run - run - run - run - a - way.
C7
2
run - a - way.

SEA OF LOVE

featured in the Motion Picture SEA OF LOVE

Words and Music by GEORGE KHOURY
and PHILIP BAPTISTE

G
C
To Coda
1
G
love you.
love you.
2
G
D
C
Come with me
D
C
B7
to the sea of
D.C. al Coda
D
D7
love.
CODA
G
N.C.

E♭
3fr
D♭
Come with me
E♭
3fr
D♭
to the sea
C7
E♭
3fr
E♭7
A♭
4fr
of love. Come with me,
C7
D♭
my love, to the sea, the

Bb7
Ab
4fr
sea of love.
I want to tell you
Bb7
Ab
Db
just how much I love you.
Ab
I want to tell you,
Bb7
Ab
Db
Ab
oh, how much I love you.
rit.

SEE YOU LATER, ALLIGATOR

Words and Music by
ROBERT GUIDRY

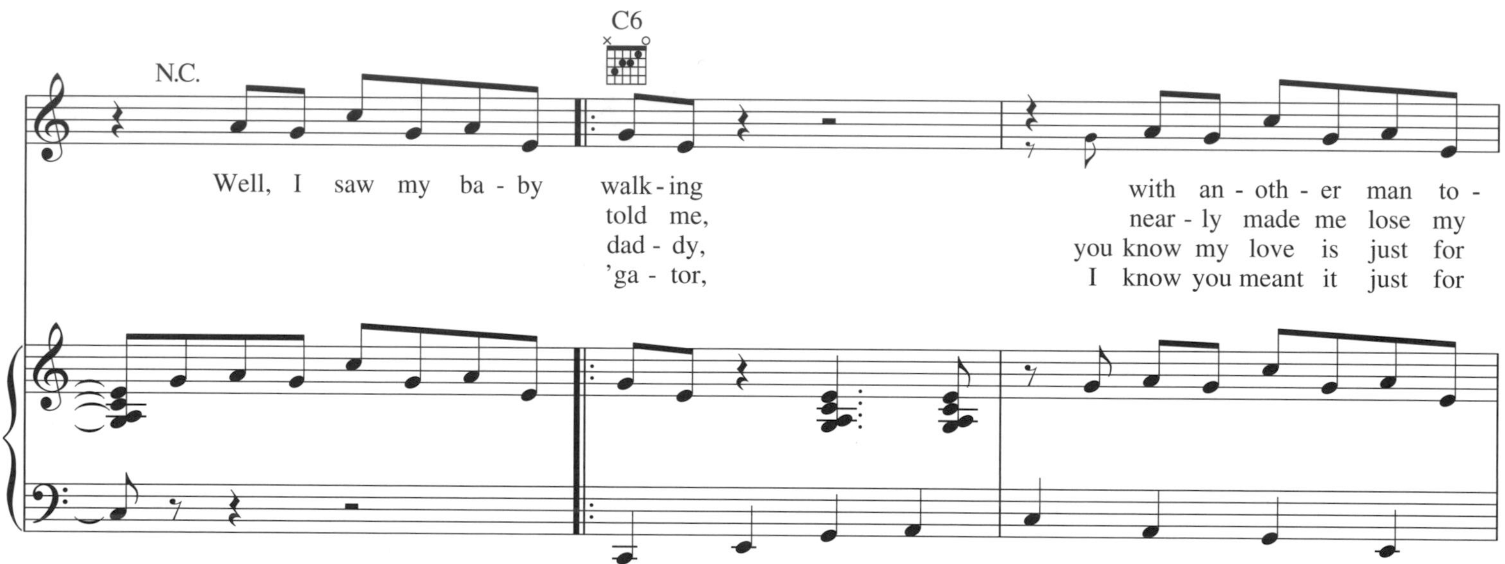

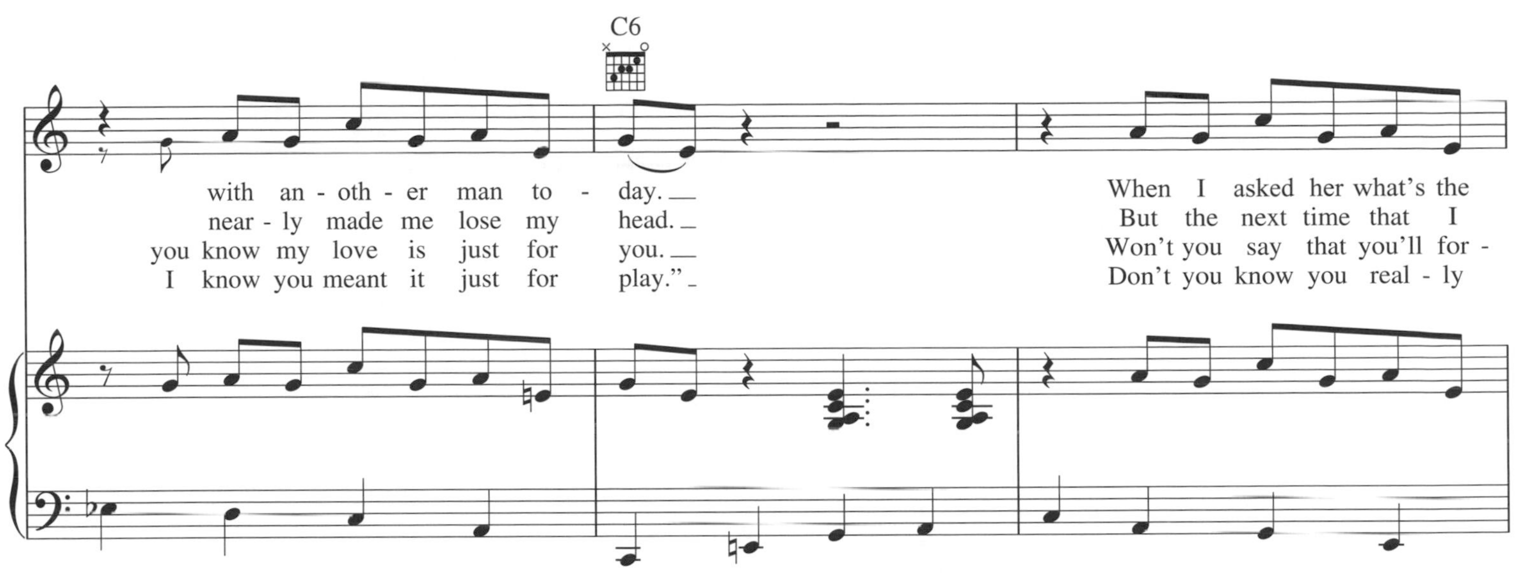
C6
with an - oth - er man to - day.
near - ly made me lose my head.
you know my love is just for you.
I know you meant it just for play."
When I asked her what's the
But the next time that I
Won't you say that you'll for -
Don't you know you real - ly

G7
C6
mat - ter, this is what I heard her say:
saw her, re - mind - ed her of what she said.
give me, and say your love for me is true?"
hurt me, and this is what I have to say:

N.C.
C6
"See you lat - er, al - li - ga - tor,
af - ter 'while, croc - o -
3

C7
F9
dile; __ see you lat - er, al - li - ga - tor,
C6
af - ter 'while, __ croc - o - dile. __ Can't you see you're in my
G7
way now? Don't you know you cramp my
1-3
C6
style?"
N.C.
When I thought of what she
She said, "I'm sor - ry, pret - ty
I said, "Wait a min - ute,
4
C6
D♭6/9
C6/9
style?" __

SINGING THE BLUES

Words and Music by
MELVIN ENDSLEY

F
B♭
F
nev - er felt more like cry - ing all night 'cause ev - 'ry - thing's wrong and
C7
B♭
C7
noth - ing ain't right with - out you. You got me sing - ing the
F
F7
B♭
F
blues. The moon and stars no long - er shine, the
B♭
F
B♭
F
dream is gone I thought was mine. There's noth - ing left for me to do but

C7
F
cry ___ o - ver you. ___ Well, I nev - er felt more like
B♭
F
C7
run - ning a - way, ___ but why should I go, ___ 'cause I could - n't stay ___ with -
B♭
C7
1
F
B♭
out you. You got me sing - ing the blues. ___
F
C
2
F
C7
F
___ Well, I blues. ___

THE SHOOP SHOOP SONG
(It's in His Kiss)

Words and Music by
RUDY CLARK

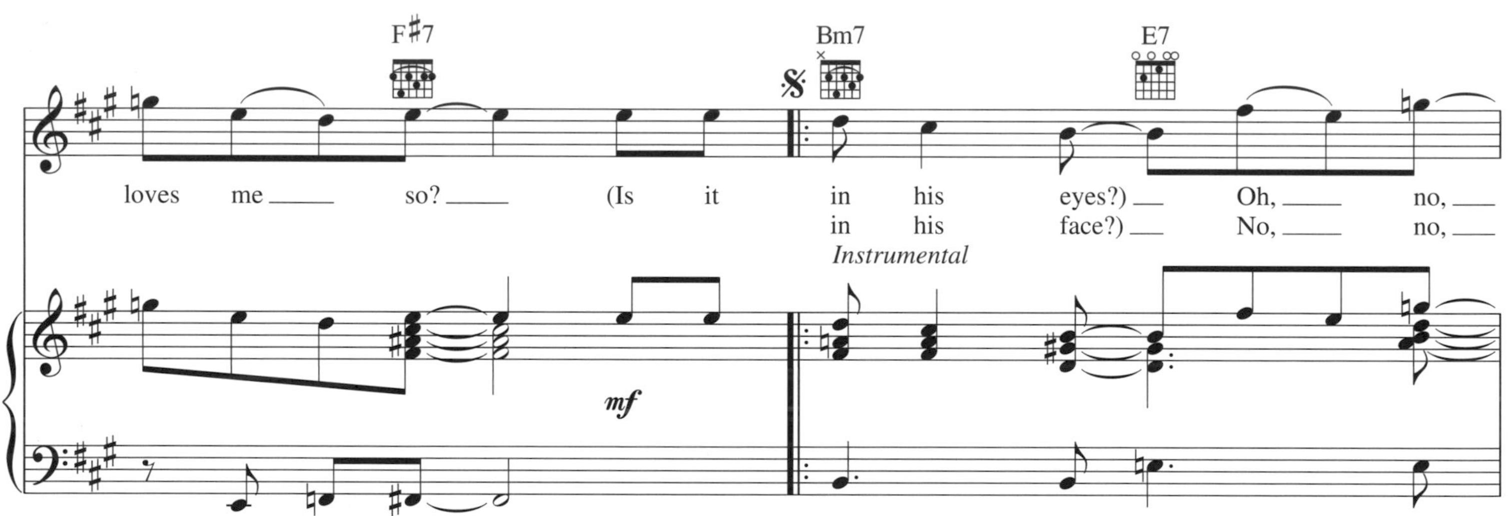

A
F♯m
Bm7
E7
A
D
wan - na know if he loves you so, it's in his kiss.
wan - na know if he loves you so, it's in his kiss.
(That's where it is.)

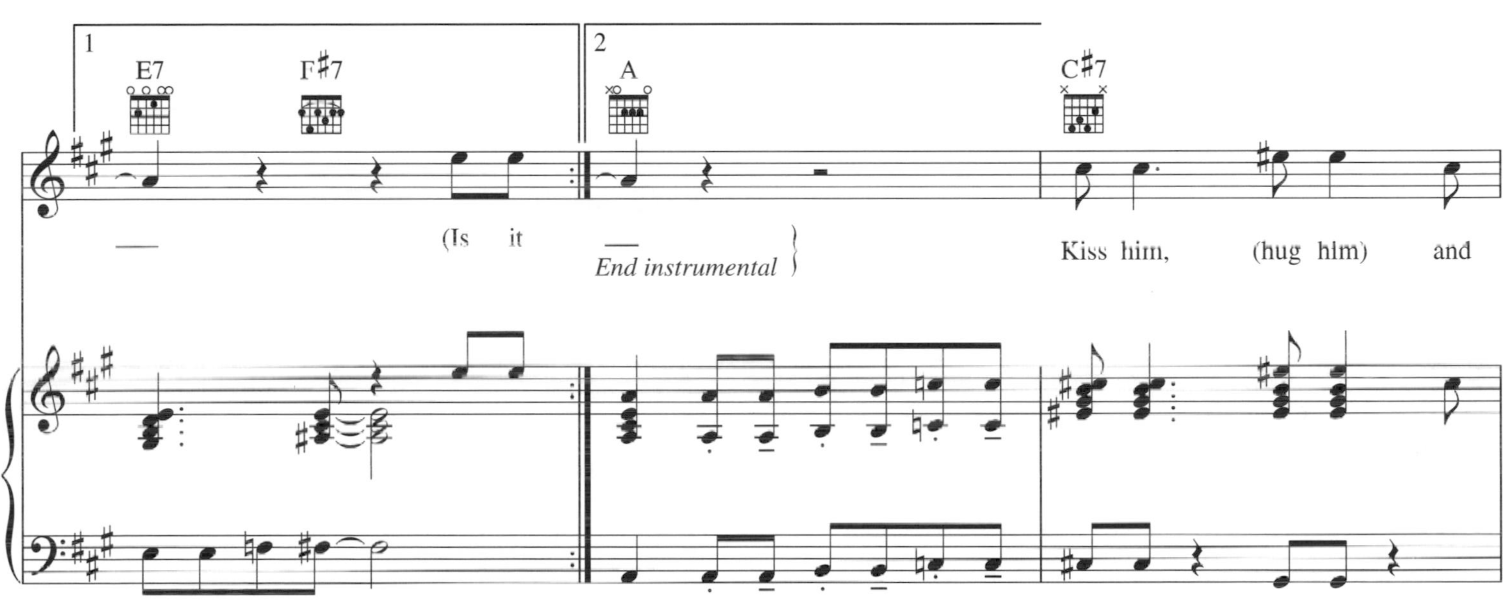
1
2
E7
F♯7
A
C♯7
(Is it
End instrumental
Kiss him, (hug him) and

F♯m7
squeeze him tight, and find out what you wan - na know.

B7
E7
If it's love, if it real - ly is, it's there in his

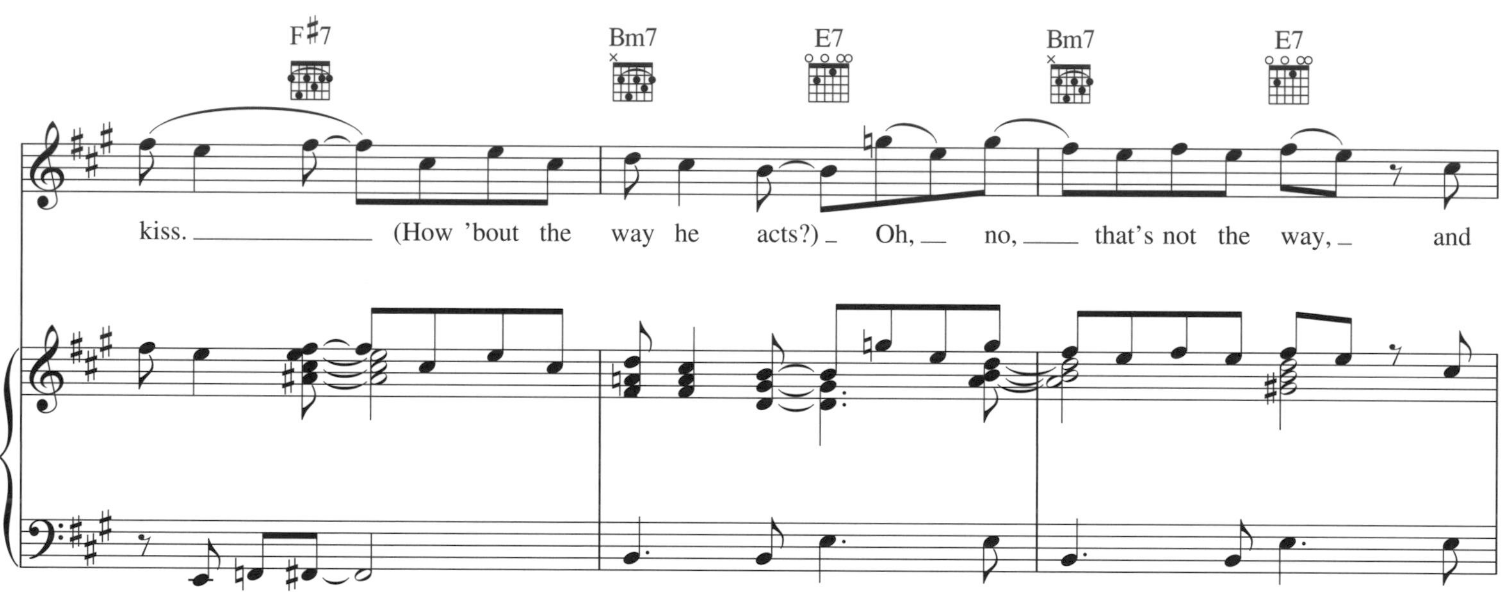
F♯7
Bm7
E7
Bm7
E7
kiss. (How 'bout the way he acts?) Oh, no, that's not the way, and

Bm7
E7
Bm7
E7
A
F♯m
you're not lis - t'nin' to all that I say. If you wan - na know if he

To Coda
Bm7
E7
A
D
loves you so, it's in his kiss.

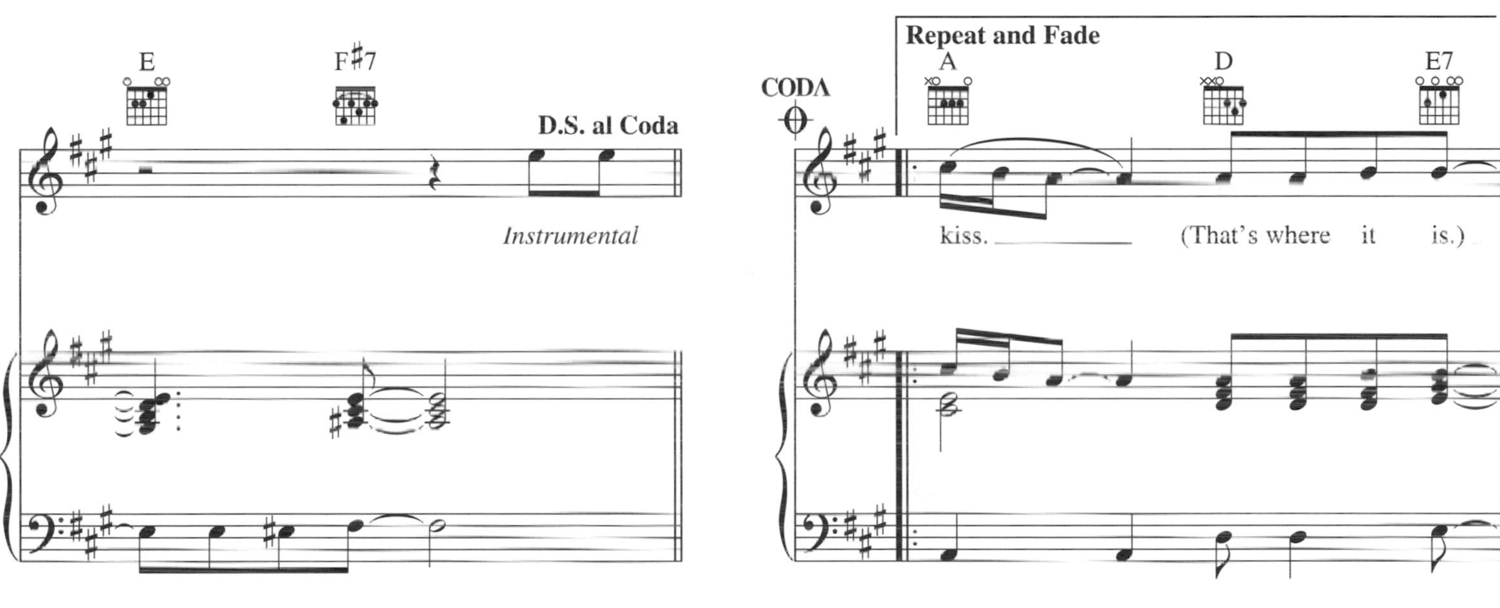
E
F#7
D.S. al Coda
Instrumental
CODA
Repeat and Fade
A
D
E7
kiss. (That's where it is.)

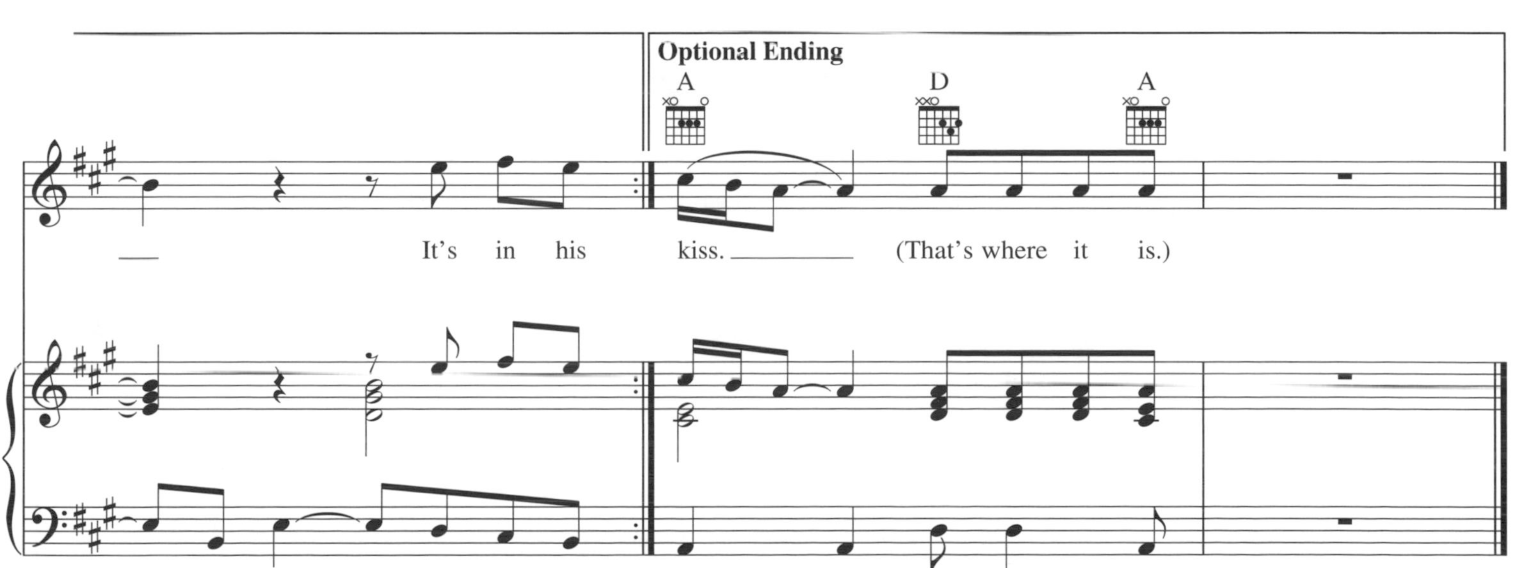
Optional Ending
A
D
A
It's in his kiss. (That's where it is.)

SHOP AROUND

Words and Music by BERRY GORDY
and WILLIAM "SMOKEY" ROBINSON

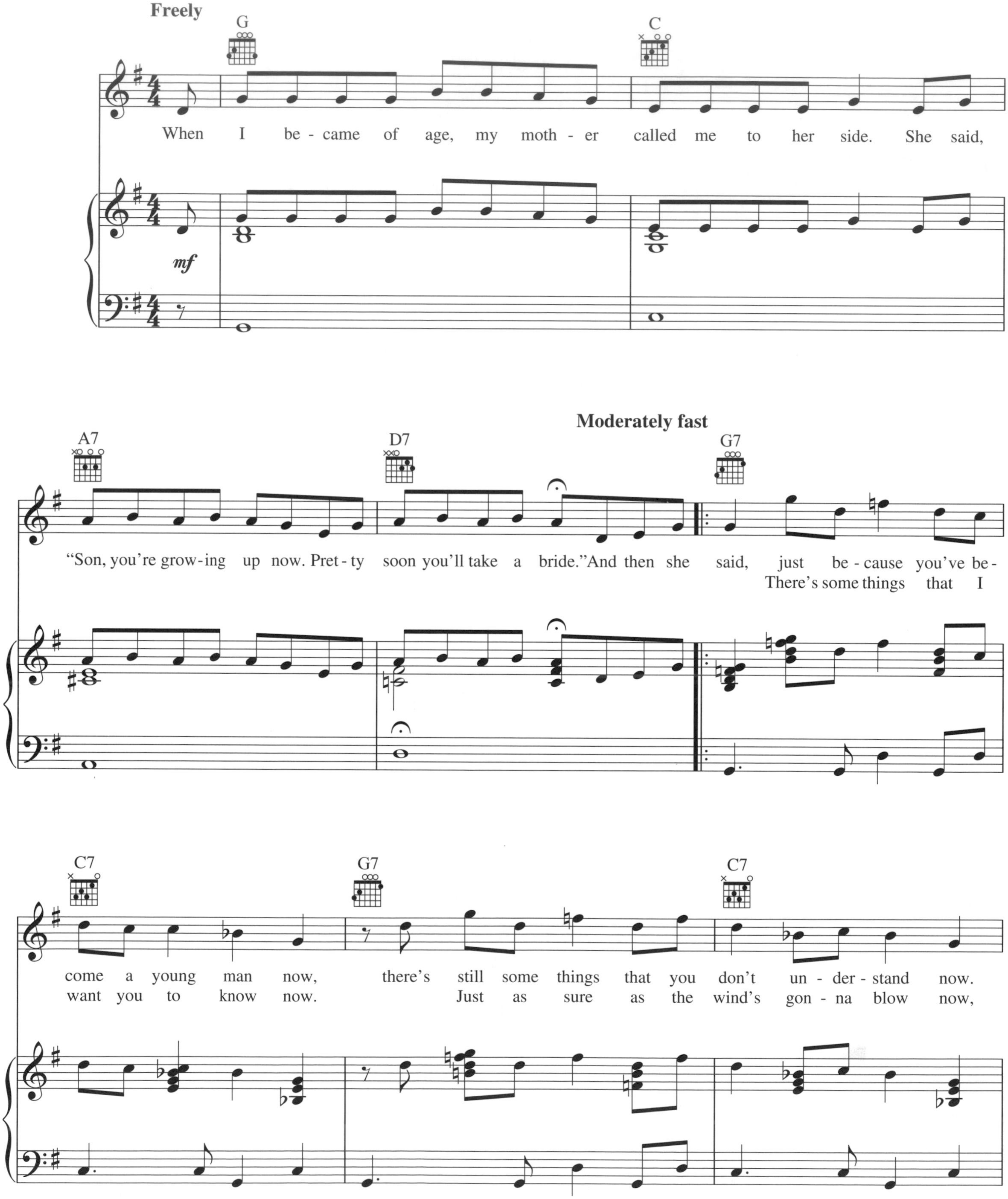

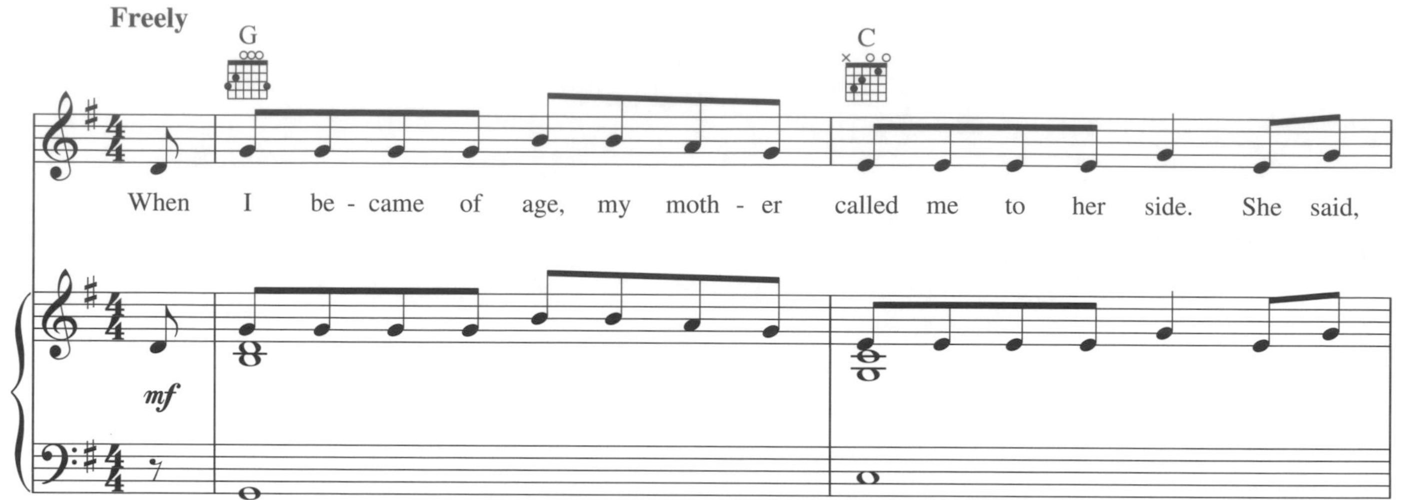

A7 D7 **Moderately fast** G7

"Son, you're grow-ing up now. Pret - ty soon you'll take a bride."And then she said, just be - cause you've be -
There's some things that I

C7 G7 C7

come a young man now, there's still some things that you don't un - der - stand now.
want you to know now. Just as sure as the wind's gon - na blow now,

G7
C7
G7
Be - fore you ask some girl for her hand now, keep your free - dom for as
the wom - en come and the wom - en gon - na go now, be - fore you tell 'em that you
C7
A7
D7
G7
long as you can now.
love 'em so now.
My ma - ma told me you bet - ter shop a - round, oh
C7
G7
1
D7
yeah, you bet - ter shop a - round. Ah.
2
D7
C7
Try to get your - self a bar - gain, son. Don't

G7
C7
be sold on the very first one.
Pret - ty girls come a
A7
N.C.
D7
dime a doz - en. A - try to find one who's gon - na give you true lov - in'.
G7
C7
G7
Be - fore you take a girl and say I do now, make sure she's in
C7
To Coda
A7
D7
N.C.
G7
love with you now. My ma - ma told me you bet - ter shop a - round.
3

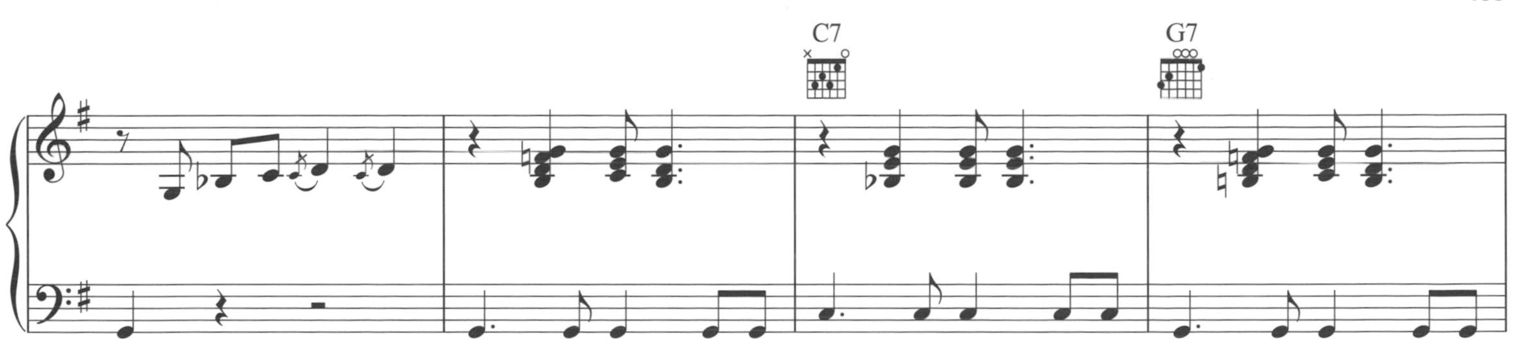
C7
G7

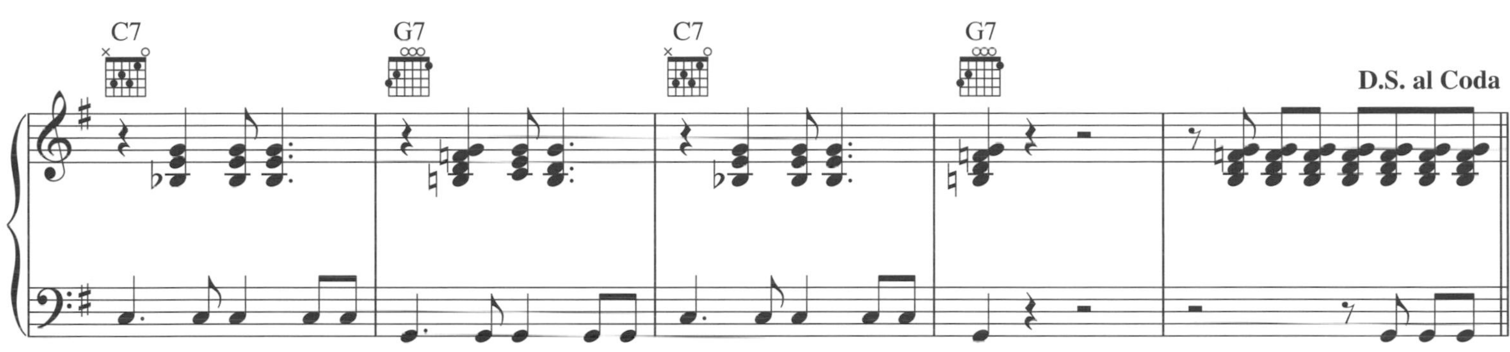
C7
G7
C7
G7
D.S. al Coda

CODA
G7
C7
G7
C7
Make sure that her love is true now, I hate to see you feel-in' sad and blue now.

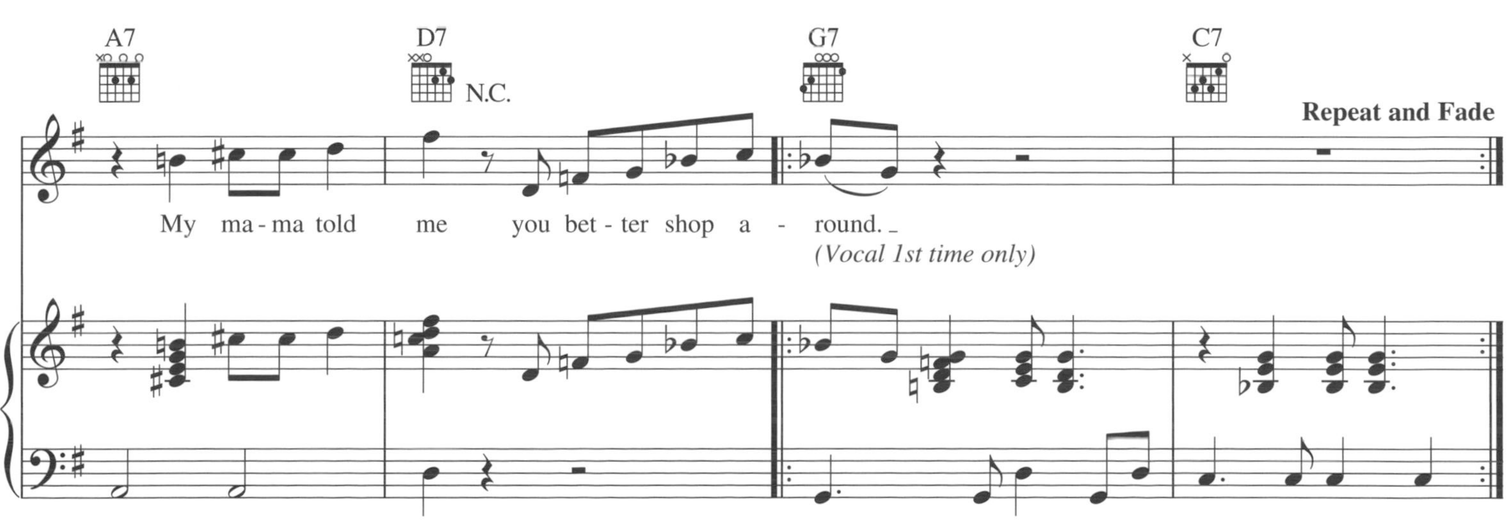
A7
D7
N.C.
G7
C7
Repeat and Fade
My ma-ma told me you bet-ter shop a - round.
(Vocal 1st time only)

SHOUT

Words and Music by O'KELLY ISLEY,
RONALD ISLEY and RUDOLPH ISLEY

Dm
F
say you will.
Don't for - get to
Dm
F
say yeah, yeah, yeah, yeah, yeah.
Say
Dm
F
you will. Say it right now, ba - by. Say
Dm
F
you will. Come on, come on.
Say

Dm
F
you will hey, hey, hey. Say
Dm
F
you will. Come on now.
(Say) Say that you
(Say) Say that you
Dm
F
love me. (Say) Say that you need me. (Say) Come
want me. (Say) You wan - na please me.
Dm
F
on, now. (Say) Come on, now. (Say) Come

Dm
N.C.
F
on, now. (Say.) I still re - mem - ber (Shoo - by
Dm
doo - wop.) when you used to be nine years old (Shoo - by -
F
doo.) yeah, yeah. I was a fool for you
Dm
from the bot - tom of my soul,

F
yeah. Now that you've grown up
Dm
you're old e - nough to know,
F
yeah, yeah. You wan - na leave me. (Shoo - by
Dm
doo - wop.) You wan - na let me go. (Shoo - by

Swing
(♩♩ = ♩♪)
N.C.
F7
doo - wop, doo - wop.) I want you to know.
I said I want you to know right now, yeah. You've been good to me
ba - by, bet - ter than I've been to my - self, yeah, hey.
And if you ev - er leave me I don't want no - bod - y else,

hey, hey. I said I want you to know, hey.
Original tempo
I said I want you to know right now, yeah, yeah. You know you
make me wan - na (Shout!)
(w/lead vocal ad lib.)
F
Dm
(Shout!)
Play 7 times
F
N.C.
(Shout!)
Freely
Now wait a

F
Bb/F
min - ute. I feel all
F
Bb/F
F
F7
right. (Yeah, yeah, yeah, yeah, yeah, yeah.) Now that I've got my wom-an, I feel all
Bb7
right. (Yeah, yeah, yeah, yeah, yeah.) Ev-'ry time I think a-bout you.
Original tempo
You been so good to me. You know you make me wan - na

F
Dm
(Shout!) lift my hands up and (Shout!) throw my head back and
F
Dm
(Shout!) pick my hands up and (Shout!) come on now.
F
Dm
(Shout!) Take it eas - y. (Shout!) Take it eas - y.
F
Dm
(Shout!) Take it eas - y. (Shout!) A lit - tle bit

F
soft - er now. (Shout!) A lit - tle bit soft - er now.
decresc.
Dm
Play 8 times
F
(Shout!) A lit - tle bit soft - er now. (Shout!) A lit - tle bit
cresc.
Dm
Play 6 times
F
loud - er now. (Shout!) A lit - tle bit loud - er now. (Shout!) Hey,
Dm
F
hey. (Hey, hey.) Hey,

Dm
F
hey.
(Hey,
hey.)
Hey.
Dm
F
(Hey.)
Hey.
Dm
F
(Hey.)
Shout
now.
Dm
F
Jump up and shout now.
Jump up and shout now.

Dm
F
Jump up and shout now. Ev - 'ry - bod - y shout now.
Ev - 'ry - bod - y shout now. Ev - 'ry - bod - y shout, shout,
Repeat and Fade
shout, shout, shout, shout, shout, shout. Shout, shout,
Optional Ending
shout, shout. Shout, shout, shout, shout. Shout.

SIXTEEN CANDLES

Words and Music by LUTHER DIXON
and ALLYSON R. KHENT

E♭
E♭maj7
E♭7
A♭
can - dles,
make your wish come true,
for I'll be
B♭7
Fm7
B♭7
E♭
A♭
wish - ing
that you love me, too.
E♭9
E♭7
A♭
A6
A♭
B♭7
You're on - ly six - teen,
but you're my teen - age
E♭6
B♭m
C7
queen.
You're the pret - ti - est, love - li - est

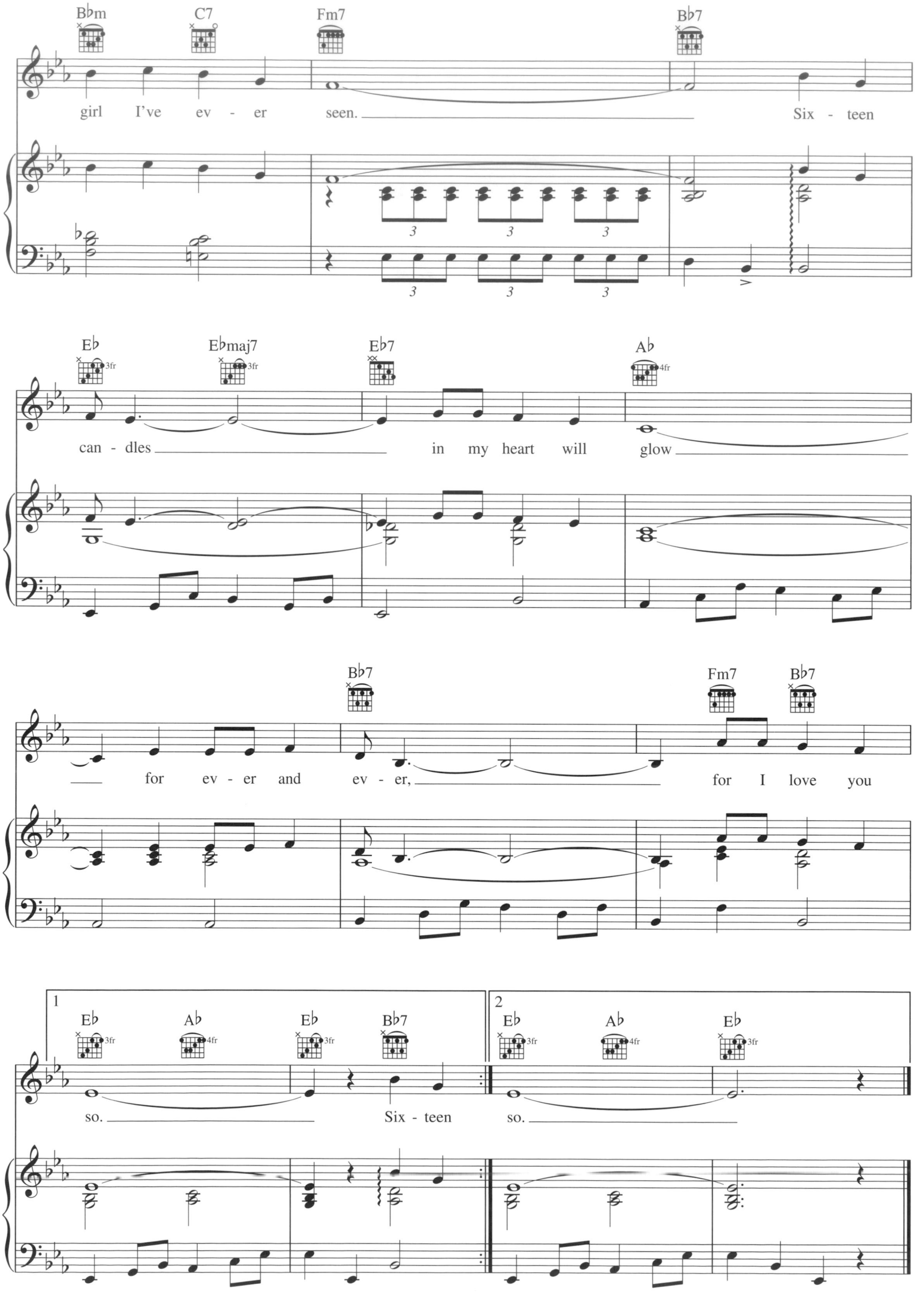

B♭m C7 Fm7 B♭7

girl I've ev - er seen. Six - teen

E♭ E♭maj7 E♭7 A♭

can - dles in my heart will glow

B♭7 Fm7 B♭7

for ev - er and ev - er, for I love you

1 E♭ A♭ E♭ B♭7

so. Six - teen

2 E♭ A♭ E♭

so.

SPLISH SPLASH

Words and Music by BOBBY DARIN
and MURRAY KAUFMAN

C7 F7

think - in' ev - 'ry - thing was all right. Well, I
teens ___ had the danc - in' bug. There was

B♭

stepped out the tub, put my feet on the floor. I
Lol - li - pop with Peg - gy Sue. Good

E♭6 Edim7 F7

wrapped the towel a - round me and I o - pened the door, and then, a -
gol - ly, Miss Mol - ly was a - e - ven there, too. A - well, a -

B♭ F7

- splish splash, I jumped back in the bath. ___ Well,
- splish splash, I for - got a - bout the bath. ___ I

B♭
1
how was I to know there was a par - ty go - ing on?
went and put my danc - ing shoes
2
on. I was a - splish - in' and a - splash - in', I was a -
roll - in' and a - stroll - in'.
E♭9
I was a - mov - in' and a - groov - in',
B♭
I was a - reel - in' with the feel - in'.
Repeat and Fade
I was a -
Optional Ending

SLEEPWALK

By SANTO FARINA,
JOHN FARINA and ANN FARINA

C
F
C
C7
F
Fm
C
C7
F
Fm
G7
A♭7
4fr
G7
A♭7
G7
C
Am
Fm
G7
C
Am
Fm
G7
C
Am
Fm
G7
1
C
Am
A♭7
G7
2
C
F7
C
rall.

STAGGER LEE

Words and Music by LLOYD PRICE
and HAROLD LOGAN

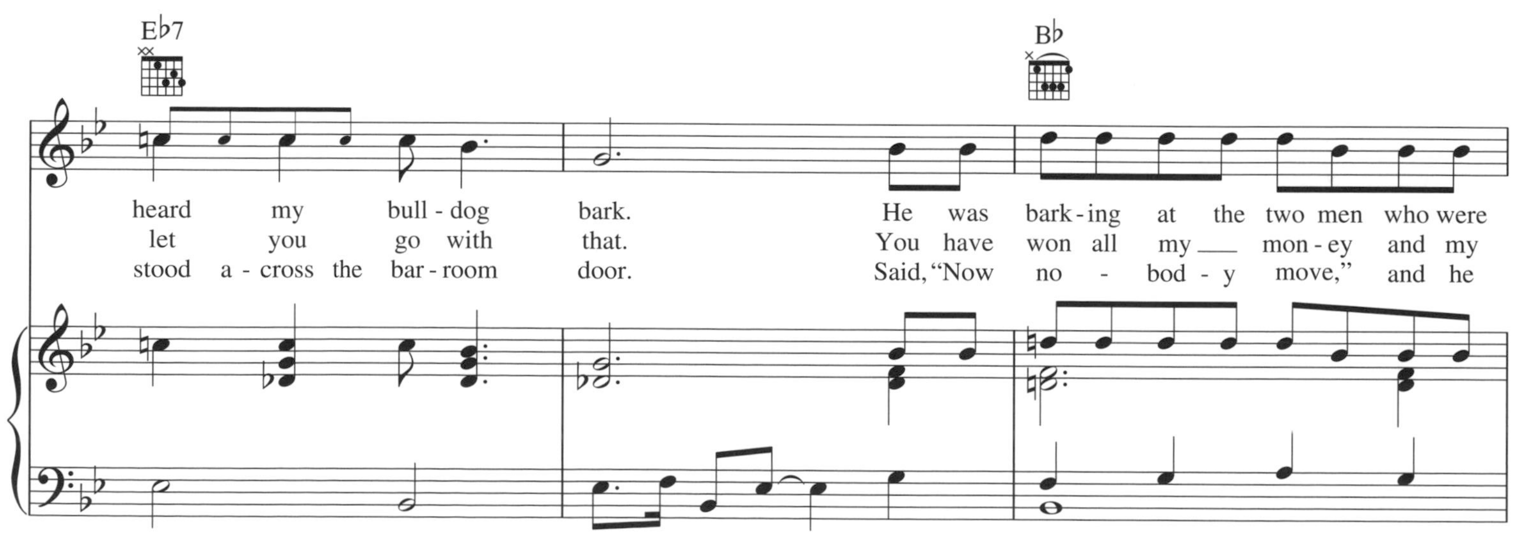

F7
B♭6
F7
F7♯5
gam - bling in the dark. It was
brand - new Stet - son hat." Stag - ger
pulled his for - ty - four. "Stag - ger
B♭
F7
B♭7
E♭7
Stag - ger Lee and Bil - ly, two men who gam - ble
Lee went home, and he got his for - ty -
Lee," cried Bil - ly, "oh please, don't take my
B♭
F7
late Stag - ger Lee threw sev - en, Bil - ly swore that he threw
four. Said, "I'm go - ing to the bar - room just to pay that debt I
life. I got three lit - tle chil - dren and a ver - y sick - ly
1, 2
B♭6
F7
F7♯5
3
B♭6
F7
F7♯5
eight. Stag - ger wife." Stag - ger
owe." Stag - ger

B♭
F7♯5
B♭7
E♭7
Lee ___ shot Bil - ly. ___ Oh, he shot that poor boy so bad, 'til the
F7
bul - let came through Bil - ly, and it broke the bar - ten - der's glass. ___ Look out now.
Go, Stag - ger Lee. Go, Stag - ger Lee. Go, Stag - ger Lee. Go, Stag - ger Lee.
B♭6
Go, Stag - ger Lee. Go, Stag - ger Lee. Go, Stag - ger Lee. Go.

STAND BY ME

Words and Music by JERRY LEIBER,
MIKE STOLLER and BEN E. KING

F
see,
sea,
oh, I won't be a - fraid
I won't cry, I won't cry
no I won't be a - fraid
no I won't shed a tear
Dm
C
Dm
just as
B♭
C
F
long as you stand, stand by me.
So dar - ling, dar - ling,
F
Dm
C
Dm
stand by me, stand by me, oh

B♭
C
F
stand, stand by me, stand by me.
1
2
If the
Darling, stand by me,
Dm
C
Dm
B♭
stand by me, oh stand,
C
F
Repeat and Fade
stand by me, stand by me. When - ev - er I'm in trou - ble, won't you

STAY

Words and Music by
MAURICE WILLIAMS

Eb
F7
Bb
Gm
3fr
Could we have an - oth - er dance, dear, just a - one more,
one more time? Oh, won't you stay
N.C.
just a lit - tle bit long - er? Please let me
dance. Please say that you will.
3

(Let Me Be Your)
TEDDY BEAR

Words and Music by KAL MANN
and BERNIE LOWE

G7
N.C.
C
be your Ted - dy Bear.
F
G7
I don't want to be your ti - ger 'cause
F
G7
F
ti - gers play too rough. I don't want to be your
G7
F
G7
C
li - on 'cause li - ons ain't the kind you love e - nough.

N.C.
C
Just wan - na be your Ted - dy Bear.
F
Put a chain a - round my neck and
C
G7
lead me an - y - where. Oh, let me be
N.C.
your Ted - dy
1
C
F7
C
G7
Bear.
2
C
F7
C
Bear.

TEQUILA

By CHUCK RIO

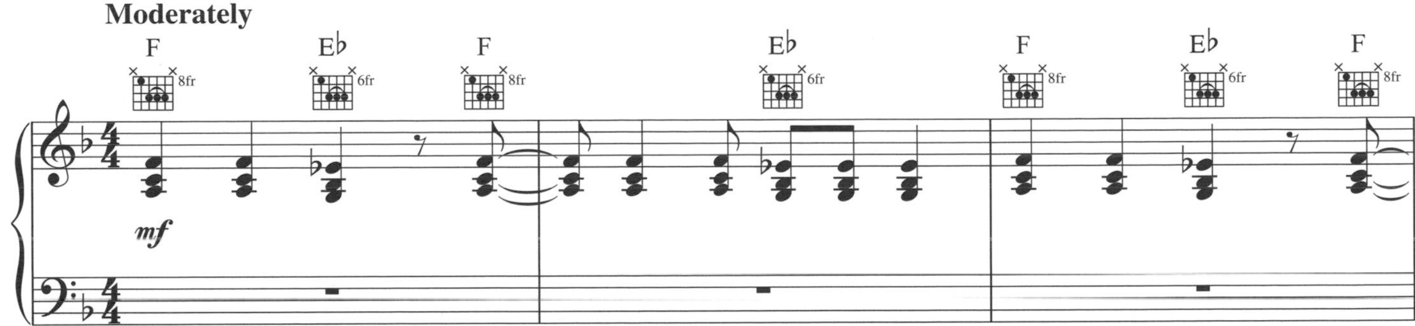

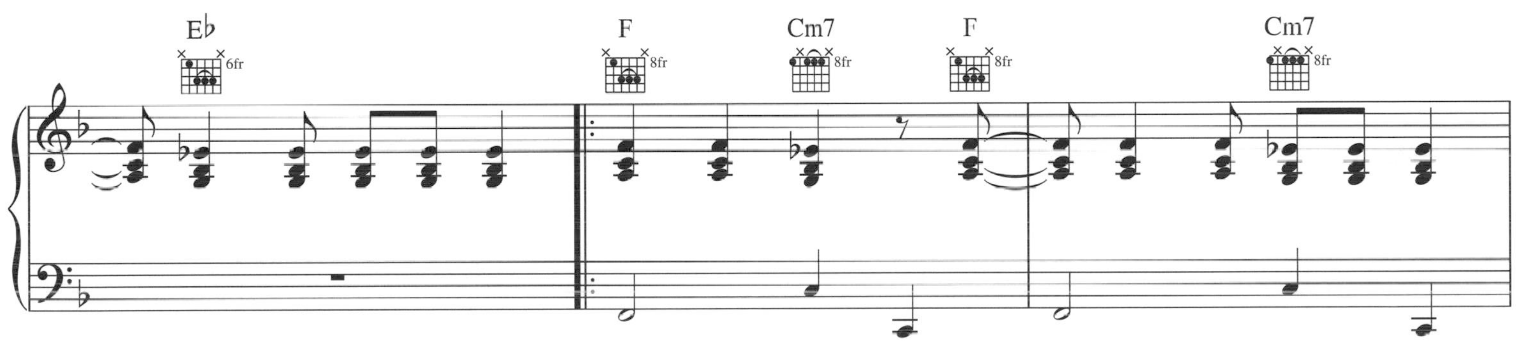

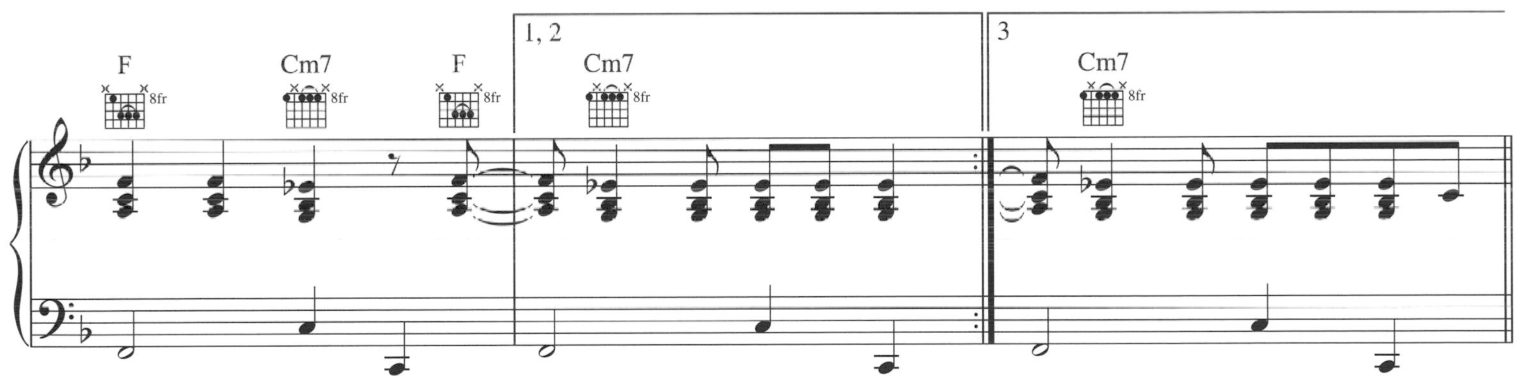

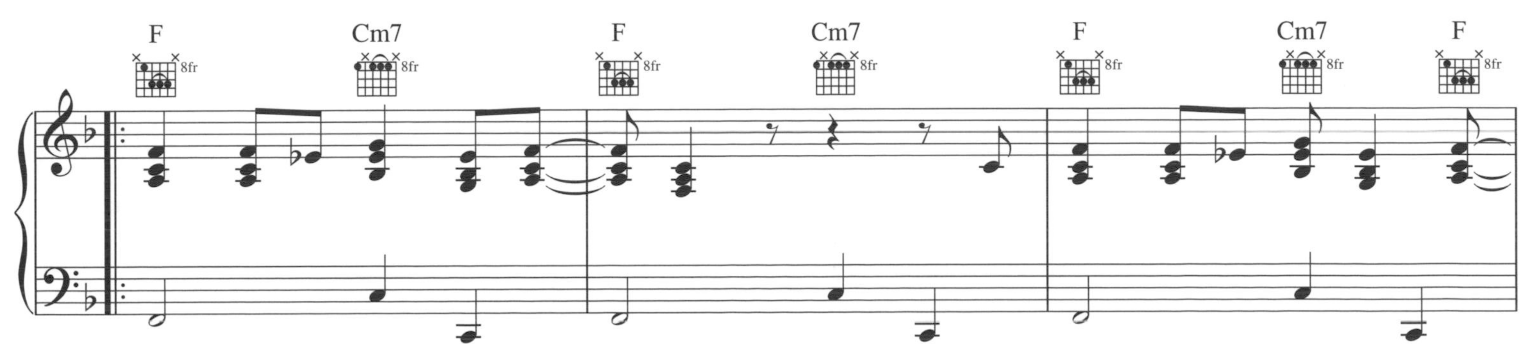

Cm7
8fr
F
8fr
Cm7
8fr
F
8fr
Cm7
8fr
F
8fr
Cm7
8fr
F
8fr
Cm7
8fr
F
8fr
Cm7
8fr
F
8fr
Cm7
8fr
F
8fr
Cm7
8fr
F
8fr
Cm7
8fr
F
8fr
Cm7
8fr
F
8fr
Cm7
8fr
F
8fr
Cm7
8fr
Fdim7
7fr
F6
8fr
Fdim7
7fr
F6
8fr
Fdim7
7fr
F6
8fr

G
C
N.C.
F
Cm7
F
8fr
(Spoken:) Tequila!
Cm7
F
Cm7
F
Cm7
F
Cm7
F
8fr
Cm7
F
Cm7
F
1
Cm7
2
Cm7
F
Cm7
F
Cm7
F
Cm7
F
Cm7
Play 3 times
F
E♭
F
E♭
F
E♭
F
6fr
(Spoken:) Tequila!

TEEN ANGEL

Words and Music by
JEAN SURREY

D7
G
Teen an - gel, can you hear me? Teen an - gel, can you see — me?
C
D7
Are you some - where up a - bove and am I still your
1, 2
G
D7
G
3
G
own — true love?
What
Just
own — true love?
Freely
Em
C
D7
G
Teen an - gel, teen an - gel, an - swer me, please.
rit.

THAT'LL BE THE DAY

Words and Music by JERRY ALLISON,
NORMAN PETTY and BUDDY HOLLY

B♭
C7
F7
un - til you tell me, may - be, that some day, well, I'll be through! Well,
E♭
3fr
that - 'll be the day, when you say, good - bye. Yes,
B♭
B♭7
E♭
that - 'll be the day, when you make me cry. Ah, you say you're gon na leave, you
B♭
N.C.
To Coda
know it's a lie, 'cause that - 'll be the day

F7
Bb
Bb7
Eb
3fr
when I die. Well,
when Cu - pid shot his dart,
Bb
Bb7
Eb
3fr
Edim
F7
Bb
Bb7
he shot it at your heart.
So if we ev - er part and
I leave you,
Eb
3fr
Bb
C7
C7b5
7fr
you say you told me an' you
told me bold - ly,
that some day, well,
D.S. al Coda
F
C9
F7
Bb7#5
6fr
I'll be through. Well,
CODA
F7
Bb
when I die.

TRAVELIN' MAN

Words and Music by
JERRY FULLER

Easy Rock

Eb Cm Eb

mf

Cm Eb Cm

I'm a trav - el - in' man and I've made a lot o' stops

mp

Eb Cm Eb Eb7

all o - ver the world; and in ev - er - y port I

Ab 4fr Eb Bb7 Eb Bb7

own the heart of at least one love - ly girl. I've a

E♭ Cm E♭
pret - ty se - ño - ri - ta wait - in' for me down in old Mex - i - co;
Guitar solo
Cm E♭ E♭7 A♭ E♭ B♭7 E♭
4fr
and if you're ev - er in A - las - ka, stop and see my cute lit - tle Es - ki - mo.
A♭ Gm A♭
4fr
Solo ends
Oh, my sweet frau - lein down in Ber - lin town makes my heart start to
3
E♭ A♭ Gm F7
4fr
yearn; and my Chi - na doll down in old Hong Kong waits for my re -

B♭7
E♭
Cm
turn. Pret - ty Pol - y - ne - sian ba - by o - ver the sea,
Cm
E♭7
A♭
4fr
I re - mem - ber the night when we walked on the sands of Wai - ki - ki and I
To Coda
B♭7
D.S. al Coda
held you, oh, so tight.
CODA
Optional Ending
Repeat and Fade
Oh,
Yes,
I'm a trav - el - in' man.
Ooh.

THERE'S A KIND OF HUSH
(All Over the World)

Words and Music by LES REED
and GEOFF STEPHENS

Moderately, with a steady beat

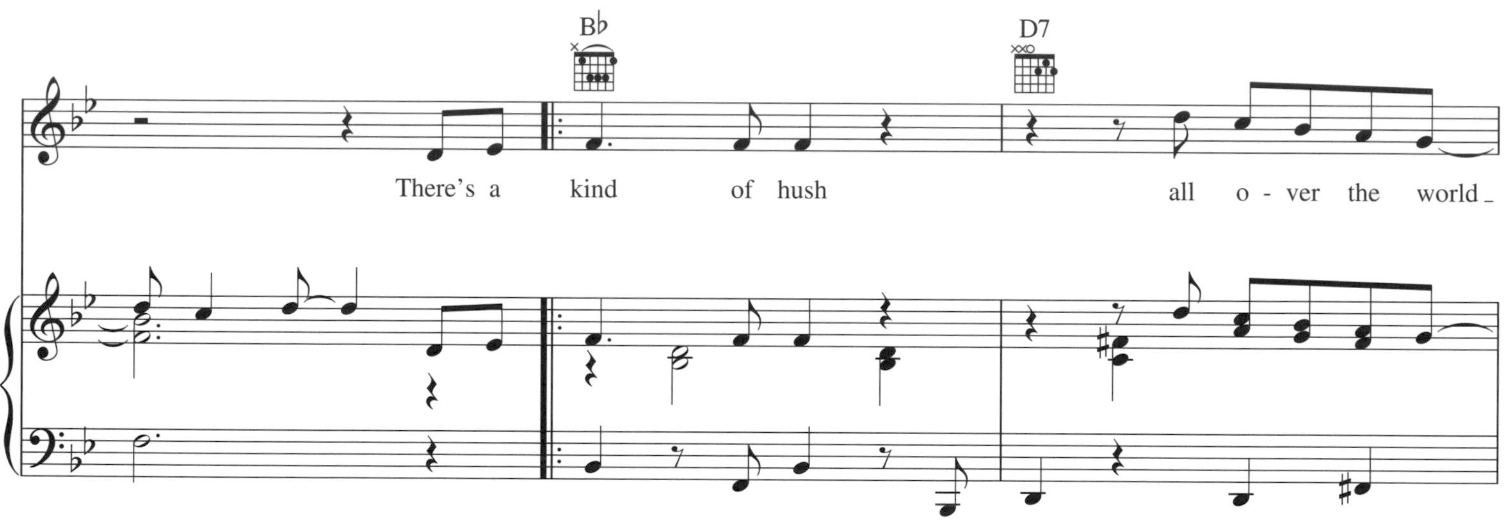

F7
Bb
F7
of lov-ers in love.
You know what I mean.
Just the
Bb
D7
Gm
3fr
two of us
an no-bod-y else
in sight.
Bb7
Eb
F7
There's no-bod-y else
and I'm feel-ing good
just hold-ing you tight.
Bb
Bb7
Eb
3fr
So lis-ten ver-y care-

E♭6
E♭maj7
E♭6
- ful - ly, closer now and you will see what I mean.
B♭
It is - n't a dream.
B♭7
E♭
E♭6
The on - ly sound that you will hear is
E♭maj7
E♭6
F7
when I whis - per in your ear, "I love you

for - ev - er and ev - er."
There's a
B♭
D7
Gm
kind of hush all o - ver the world to - night,
B♭7
E♭
F7
all o - ver the world you can hear the sounds of lov - ers in love.
1
B♭
F7
There's a
2
B♭
Cm7/F
B♭6/9

WHERE DID OUR LOVE GO

Words and Music by BRIAN HOLLAND,
LAMONT DOZIER and EDWARD HOLLAND

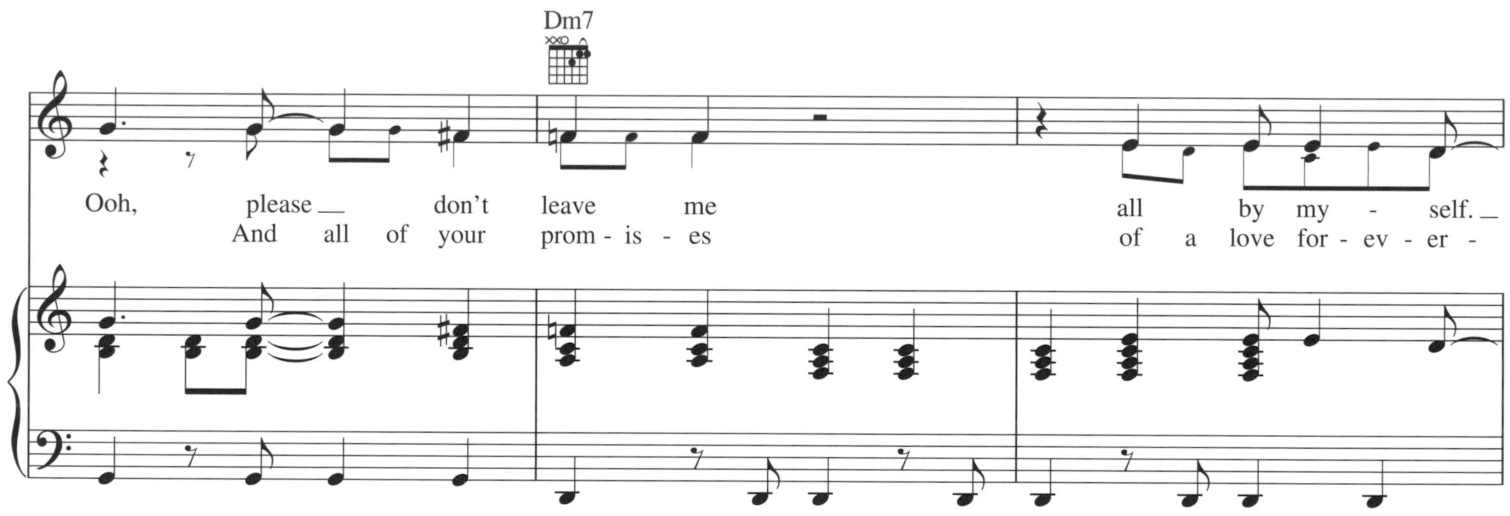

G
yearn - ing feel - in' in - side me. Ooh, deep in -
Dm
G
To Coda
side me and it hurts so bad.
F(add9)
C
3
You came in - to my heart (ba - by ba - by) so ten - der -
G
Dm7
ly with a burn - ing love (ba - by ba - by)

G
F
C
that stings like a bee. (ba - by ba - by)
Now that I sur - ren - der (ba - by ba - by)
G
Dm7
so help - less - ly,
you now want to leave. (ba - by ba - by)
G
F(add9)
C
Ooh, you wan - na leave me. (ba - by ba - by)
Ooh. (ba - by ba - by)
Ba - by, ba - by,
G
Dm7
where did our love go?
Ooh, don't you want me?

G7
F(add9)
Don't you want me no more? (ba - by ba - by) Ooh, ba - by.
C
G
Dm7
G
1
F(add9)
2
F(add9)
D.C. al Coda
CODA
F(add9)
C
Be - fore _ you won my heart, (ba - by ba - by)

G
you were a per - fect guy.
But now that you
Dm7
G
N.C.
got me, you wan - na leave me be - hind. (ba - by ba - by) Ooh, ba - by.
C
G
Ba - by, ba - by, ba - by, don't leave me. Ooh, please don't
Dm7
G
N.C.
Repeat and Fade
leave me all by my - self. (ba - by ba - by) Ooh.

A WHITE SPORT COAT
(And a Pink Carnation)

Words and Music by
MARTY ROBBINS

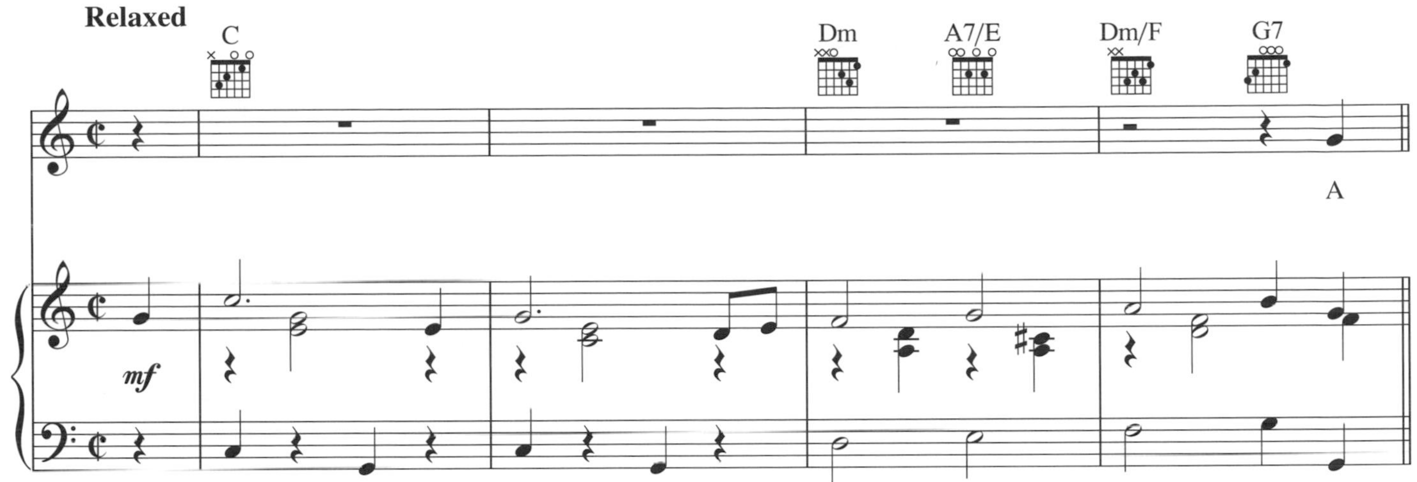

C
Dm
G7
white sport coat and a pink car - na - tion,
F
G7
C
F
C
I'm all a - lone in ro - mance.
G7
C
Once you told me long a - go
to the Prom with
D7
me you'd go.
Now you've changed your mind, it seems

G7
C
some - one else will hold my dreams. A white sport
Dm
G7
coat and a pink car - na - tion,
F
G7
1
C
C♯dim
4fr
I'm in a blue, blue mood.
Dm
G7
2
C
F
C
A mood.

YAKETY YAK

Words and Music by JERRY LEIBER
and MIKE STOLLER

G7
If you don't scrub that kitch - en floor,
Get all that gar - bage out of sight,
and when you fin - ish do - ing that,
Just tell your hood - lum friend out - side,
G7sus
C
you ain't gon - na rock 'n' roll no more. Yak - et - y
or you don't go out Fri - day night. Yak - et - y
bring in the dog and put out the cat. Yak - et - y
you ain't got time to take a ride. Yak - et - y
1-3
N.C.
yak! (Spoken:) Don't talk back. Just fin - ish clean - ing up your
yak! (Spoken:) Don't talk back. You just put on your coat and
yak! (Spoken:) Don't talk back. Don't you give me no dirt - y
4
N.C.
C
yak! (Spoken:) Don't talk back. Yak - et - y yak, yak - et - y yak!

YOUNG LOVE

Words and Music by RIC CARTEY
and CAROLE JOYNER

F G7 C Am7 F G7
ev - er in my heart. Young
love for you or for me.
C G7 F G7
love, first love, filled with true de -
C Am7 F G7 C G7 F
vo - tion. Young love, our love we share with
G7 C Am7 1 F G7 2 F G7
D.S. and Fade
deep e - mo - tion. Young

WHY DO FOOLS FALL IN LOVE

Words and Music by MORRIS LEVY
and FRANKIE LYMON

F Dm7 Gm7 C7 F Dm7 Gm7 C7 F Dm7
break of day? Why do they fall in love? Why
Gm7 C7 F Dm7 Gm7 C7 F Dm7
does the rain fall from up a - bove? Why do fools fall in love?
Gm7 C7 F B♭6 B♭m6
Why do they fall in love?
Love is a los - ing game,
Why does my heart
F F7 B♭6 B♭m6
love can be a shame. I know of a fool, you see,
skip a cra - zy beat? For I know

G7
C7
F
Dm7
Gm7
C7
for that fool is me! Tell me why,
it will reach de - feat!
tell me why!
1
2
F7
B♭
Why do fools
fall in love?